Domestic Heating Design Guide

**Organisations making up the Domestic Building Services Panel of
The Chartered Institution of Building Services Engineers**

Association of Plumbing and Heating Contractors	APHC
Chartered Institution of Building Services Engineers	CIBSE
Council for Registered Gas Installers	CORGI
Office of the Deputy Prime Minister	ODPM
Electrical Contractors Association	ECA
Electricity Association	EA
Energy Saving Trust	EST
Heating and Hotwater Information Council	HHIC
Heating and Ventilating Contractors Association	HVCA
Heating Equipment Testing and Approvals Scheme	HETAS
Institute of Domestic Heating and Environmental Engineers	IDHE
Institute of Plumbing	IoP
Manufacturers of Domestic Unvented Systems	MODUS
National Inspection Council for Electrical Installation Contracting	NICEIC
Oil Firing Technical Association	OFTEC
The Scottish and Northern Ireland Plumbing Employers Federation	SNIPEF
Underfloor Heating Manufacturers Association	UHMA
The UK Government's Housing Energy Efficiency Best Practice Programme	HEEBPp

Individual Member
George Henderson

Bodies whose titles are shown in bold type have funded and supported the Domestic Heating Design Guide project. Copies of this Guide are available from funders whose contact details are given in Appendix E.

Working Group A of the Domestic Building Services Panel is responsible for this project, including its ongoing development. Its members are:

Colin Sutherland	CIBSE	Chairman
Ian Beard	HVCA	
Bill Bucknell	IDHE	
John Byrne	CORGI	
Hywel Davies	CIBSE	
George Henderson	Individual Member	
Alan Keating	HVCA	
Marcus Millett	HHIC	
Robin Oakley	IoP	
Mike Staton	HVCA	
Roger Webb	HHIC	
Bruce Young	BRE for HEEBPp	

FOREWORD

This publication is the result of work undertaken by the Domestic Building Services Panel of the Chartered Institution of Building Services Engineers.

The Panel had identified the need for an uplift of domestic heating design standards and saw the need for an up-to-date design and specification guide covering the subject. The panel recognised that the Heating and Ventilating Contractors' Association's Domestic Heating Specification published in 1993 was the best publication available on which to base their work.

Thanks are particularly due to George Henderson, who acted as Technical Author for the Guide, and to the following members of the technical drafting group:

Ian Beard	HVCA	
John Byrne	CORGI	
Alan Keating	HVCA	
Marcus Millett	CHIC	
Robin Oakley	IoP	
Colin Sutherland	CIBSE	Chairman

Assistance was also received from Duncan Pollock of Longmill Marketing.

The Guide is intended to fit into the suite of books covering Energy Efficiency, safe use of fuel and design standards listed in Appendix C. The competent heating engineer will be familiar with these.

The achievement of high standards in any engineering undertaking is a desirable end in itself. In an undertaking with such extensive implications for energy efficiency and the environment as domestic heating, high standards become a national necessity and the unfortunate general lack of them in this field is something that cannot be tolerated.

The CIBSE Panel firmly believes that a large number of domestic heating contractors are interested in becoming more involved in the science of their trade. The Guide provides a straightforward means of achieving this without the need for previous technical training. It will also form the platform for further aids to design work, making use of electronic technology.

January 2004 Edition The issue of BSEN 12828:2003. Heating systems in buildings – Design for water based heating systems, in August 2003, has seen the withdrawal of BS 5449: Specification for forced circulation hot water central heating systems for domestic premises. The references in this Guide have been updated to take account of this. The design standards in the Guide remain those arrived at by the drafting group as being appropriate for use in the United Kingdom and the Republic of Ireland.

CONTENTS

1.0 INTRODUCTION

1.1 Objective

This Domestic Heating Specification and Design Guide has been produced to assist professional heating engineers to specify and design wet central heating systems. It provides a method of coming to agreement with the client as to what is needed and will be provided. It also provides a simple means for the practitioner who wishes to design and understand central heating systems, to do so. The method of achieving this is that originally given in the *HVCA Guide to Good Practice - Domestic Heating Specification* of 1992, which formed the starting point for the drawing up of this Guide.

1.2 Specification

It is strongly recommended that a full specification is always prepared to cover heating installation work. Material from this Guide can be used in a contractual specification if agreed by both parties involved.

1.3 Scope

This Guide is intended to be used in conjunction with other publications. Reference must always be made to the statutory requirements of the Building Regulations and Standards and the Gas (Installation and Use) Regulations. Various Government publications referring to Energy Efficiency and British Standards and Industry Standards are also referred to and these should be studied as appropriate.

This Guide covers low pressure hot water space and water heating systems using automatically controlled boilers of up to 60kW output, such as those fired by gas or oil. Both open vented and sealed systems are referred to. Domestic hot water heating systems of the open vented and unvented type are included, but this Guide does not cover the design of hot and cold water draw off pipework. A reference for a publication covering this is given in Appendix C.

Specific requirements for the installation of gas and oil fired heating equipment, including fuel storage where applicable, are provided in other publications listed in Appendix C. Outline details only are given in this Guide.

1.4 Installation

This Guide does not specifically cover installation work, but would assume that the standards of the Scottish and National Vocational Qualifications are needed to comply with its quality requirements for heating system installation, and those of CORGI and OFTEC for combustion appliance installation and fuel storage matters.

2.0 ABBREVIATIONS

2.1 Abbreviations

The abbreviations used to denote components in system diagrams in this Guide are as follows:

AAV	Automatic Air Vent	**MPV**	Mid Position Valve
ABV	Automatic By-pass Valve	**MV**	Mixing Valve
AV	Air Vent	**NRV**	Non-Return Valve
B	Boiler	**OS**	Outside Sensor
BC	Boiler Controls	**OSV**	Open safety vent pipe
CF	Cold feed pipe	**OV**	Open vent pipe
CF&V	Combined feed & vent pipe	**PG&T**	Pressure Gauge & Thermometer
CT	Cylinder Thermostat	**PR**	Programmer (two or more Outputs)
CYL	Indirect Hot Water Cylinder	**PRV**	Pressure Regulating Valve
DIV	Diverting Valve	**PTRV**	Pressure & Temperature Relief Valve
DNRV	Double Non-return Valve		
DV	Drain Valve	**R**	Radiator or other Emitter
ERV	Expansion Relief Valve	**RT**	Room Thermostat
EV	Expansion Vessel	**RV**	Regulating Valve
F&E	Feed & Expansion pipe	**SV**	Stop Valve
F&EC	Feed & Expansion cistern	**TD**	Tundish
FS	Flow Sensor	**TRV**	Thermostatic Radiator Valve
HC	Heating Circulator	**TS**	Time Switch (single output)
HWB	Hot Water Blending Valve	**TSU**	Thermal Storage Unit
HWC	Hot Water Circulator	**TSV**	Temperature Safety Valve
IS	Inside Sensor	**TU**	Top-up Unit
IV	Isolating Valve	**UHWC**	Unvented Hot Water Cylinder
LSV	Radiator Lock Shield Valve	**WV**	Radiator Wheel Valve
MBV	Motorised Blending Valve	**ZV**	Zone Valve (normally closed)

3.0 ESTABLISHING THE CLIENT'S REQUIREMENTS

3.1   General Requirements

A discussion with the client should take place to ensure that the client's requirements and preferences are understood and that they are taken into account in developing the system specification.   Important decisions may have to be taken at this stage, including choice of fuel, type and location of boiler, and whether or not to retain parts of an existing system.

3.2   Fuel Choice

The choice of fuel is important, particularly because of its effect on running cost. However, that choice may be constrained by the unavailability of mains gas, or by the space available for fuel storage and access for delivery of heating oil or liquefied petroleum gas (LPG). Make clear the need to comply with gas safety regulations and the relevant parts of building regulations[1], including the provision of combustion air for heating appliances, the siting of flues and requirements for fuel storage.   Section 20 summarises the requirements for fuel storage.

Discuss fuel choice options with the client, ensuring that he or she is fully aware of the range of available options.   The costs associated with particular fuels should also be explained, including both capital costs and running costs.   Table 3.1 below shows the number of kWh in a typical delivery unit for each fuel; to compare prices divide the unit price in pence by the factor shown in the third column.

Fuel	Typical delivery unit	Number of kWh in unit
Gas and electricity	kWh	1
Heating oil (Class C2 kerosene)	Litre	10.35
Heating oil (Class D gas oil)	Litre	10.85
LPG (Propane)	Litre	7.11
Solid fuels	50 kg	420 to 480

TABLE 3.1 (source: Sutherland Associates Comparative Domestic Heating Costs)

Where gas meters are located in a remote position, it should be pointed out that the gas entry into each dwelling must be provided with an identified gas isolating valve.

---

[1] References to 'building regulations' refer to the relevant parts of the particular building regulations that apply in England and Wales, Scotland, Northern Ireland and the Irish Republic. See Appendix 'A' for a list of relevant parts of the respective regulations. References to 'gas safety regulations' apply to the 'Gas Safety (Installation and Use) Regulations' and corresponding legislation in the Irish Republic.

7

3.3　Heating Requirements

Discuss heating requirements with the client. Establish which rooms are to be heated at which times, the temperatures required, and any special needs such as may be required for the frail and elderly. Where an existing installation is being replaced or upgraded, try to obtain feedback on how it performs, as this can give useful pointers to where improvements may be needed.

3.4　Ventilation

An adequate supply of ventilation air is required to maintain air quality but excessive ventilation leads to unnecessary heat loss. Building regulations set minimum requirements for ventilation in habitable rooms. Heat losses arising from ventilation are described in Section 7 of this Guide.

The need to supply combustion air to conventionally flued heating appliances is also covered in building regulations, with the aim of ensuring effective combustion and flue operation. In particular, it is necessary to avoid combustion products being released back into the room when an extractor fan is installed in the same room as an appliance with a conventional flue. Section 19 of this Guide deals with combustion air requirements. Specific guidance is given in the CORGI publication *Essential Gas Safety* and the OFTEC publication *Technical Note TI/ 112*.

3.5　Boiler

Consider the options for boilers, taking account of the expected heating load, possible restrictions on siting, the length of pipe runs required and, where relevant, the need to couple to existing system components. If a combination boiler is to be fitted, ensure that the pressure and flow available from the cold water mains is adequate, even at times of peak demand. The choice of domestic hot water system is strongly connected to the choice of boiler. Refer to Section 12 of this guide for a description of the characteristics of hot water supplies.

The overall efficiency of the heating system is determined to a large extent by the efficiency of the boiler itself. Boilers with high efficiency should be used because fuel economy is an important requirement. Refer to Section 4 for guidance on boiler efficiency.

3.6　Boiler and Flue Location

A number of factors need to be considered in deciding the location of boilers and flues:
- access to an external wall or roof, especially for room-sealed appliances
- the supply of combustion air for conventionally flued appliances
- ventilation around the boiler casing
- access for servicing and maintenance
- provision for safe discharge from boiler safety valves
- the need for a condensate drain (for condensing boilers)

- the acceptability of pluming at the flue (for condensing boilers)
- the acceptability of expected noise levels (for pressure jet boilers)
- manufacturers' recommendations for the installation of particular boilers
- compliance with building and safety regulations.

3.7 Heat Emitters and their Location

The types and locations of heat emitters should be established, taking account of the probable layout of furniture, which could affect the height and length of the units. Placing radiators below windows is normally recommended to reduce cold down draughts, although this may be less important when windows are double glazed and inappropriate where radiators would be covered by full-length heavy drape curtains. Also, radiators placed near external doors may help offset the flow of cold air into the building.

Where space for radiators is limited, consider the use of fan convectors, which give high output from compact units and trench heating. Underfloor heating can eliminate siting problems and is ideal where low surface temperatures are required, for example for elderly or infirm occupants.

3.8 Pipework

Discuss the materials to be used, the different ways in which pipework can be routed and installed, and whether pipes should be concealed or exposed. Remember that all pipework runs in solid floors must be put in purpose-built trenches with a removable cover. Also gas and oil pipework must be installed in accordance with the relevant standards.

3.9 Controls

The function and benefits of heating system controls should be explained to the client, including their effect on comfort and running costs. Find out if there are any special requirements, such as the need to heat part of the house to a higher temperature or at different times from the rest.

Control systems are described in detail in Section 18.

3.10 Domestic Hot Water

Establish the client's requirements for hot water and how they can be provided by the system. Average hot water requirements may be assessed from the number of occupants in the dwelling but the need for special requirements should be explored, including the need for balanced hot and cold water pressures or high water pressure where mixer fittings and showers are to be used. Check that the water supply provides adequate dynamic pressure and flow if a combination boiler or thermal store is to be considered.

Explain the different characteristics of standard and combination boilers for providing domestic hot water. It may also be appropriate to explain the relative merits of unvented cylinders, thermal storage units and open vented cylinders.

Refer to Section 12 for more detail on the choice of hot water systems.

3.11 Plumbing Services

The location of cisterns, the hot water cylinder (where applicable) and hot and cold water pipework services should be agreed. All plumbing services must comply with water regulations and building regulations with regard to the positioning and insulation of equipment and pipework.

3.12 Existing Systems

Where there is an existing heating system in the property, it should be established whether any of it is to be incorporated into the new system, taking account of the suitability and sizing of existing components.

The use of new equipment on an existing system should be carefully considered to ensure compatibility. A low water content boiler should not, for example, be used with gravity circulation unless specifically permitted by its manufacturer.

Existing systems should be flushed and cleaned before new equipment is installed and care should be taken with aggressive chemicals when cleaning older systems. Strainers should be fitted to ensure that sludge from existing system components is not transferred to new boilers. The client should be advised of any possible complications.

3.13 Energy Efficiency

Opportunities to improve energy efficiency should be considered and discussed with the client, as it may be more economical to carry them out at the same time as work on the heating system. Improvements may be made to thermal insulation, boiler efficiency and heating controls, generally resulting in both fuel cost savings and improved comfort. Improvements to thermal insulation should be considered before starting on detailed system design as they can substantially reduce design heat loads and affect the sizing of both radiators and boilers. The Building Regulations for England and Wales and Scotland place mandatory energy efficiency requirements on heating systems. In England and Wales these apply to replacement systems in existing buildings as well as to new systems. References to the Building Regulations are given on page 110.

Energy efficiency is discussed in some detail in Section 4.

4.0 ENERGY EFFICIENCY

4.1 What Energy Efficiency means

The energy efficiency of a dwelling depends upon how well it is insulated and how well the heating is controlled, as well the efficiency with which its heating and hot water systems can convert fuel to heat.

The fabric of the dwelling has an important influence on the amount of energy required to keep it comfortable. If the building is badly insulated, even the most efficient heating system will require a great deal of energy to keep it warm. Overall, an energy efficient dwelling is one that is well insulated, has an efficient boiler and good heating controls. Although it may not always be possible to improve building fabric insulation, the heating installer should be aware of opportunities for improved insulation and bring them to the client's attention. Better insulation will generally improve comfort and client satisfaction and may lead to opportunities for a more competitive quotation.

Hot water systems should be insulated to minimise heat loss from storage cylinders and primary circuits; heat output from them may contribute to space heating requirements in the winter but in summer it is wasted and may make the house uncomfortably warm.

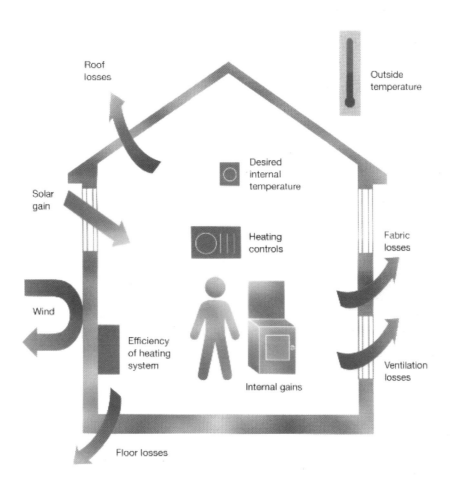

4.2 Environmental Impact

The burning of fossil fuels, such as gas, oil and coal, is responsible for a large proportion of all carbon dioxide (CO_2) emissions to the atmosphere. The concentration of CO_2 in the global atmosphere has risen by about 30% since the start of the industrial revolution. Over the past 15 years, climatologists and others have formed a consensus view that the 'greenhouse effect' arising from CO_2 and other man-made gases in the atmosphere is likely to cause global warming and consequent changes to climates around the world. This has led to agreements reached under the auspices of the United Nations Organisation to limit further emissions of greenhouse gases.

By 2010, the United Kingdom is committed to reducing its greenhouse gas emissions to 12.5% below the 1990 level. The household sector currently accounts for about a quarter of all UK CO_2 emissions and energy efficiency measures applied in the sector are expected to contribute a similar proportion of the necessary reductions. Reductions will be achieved by better insulation in new and existing houses, more efficient and better controlled heating systems, and improvements to electrical appliances.

4.3 Primary and Delivered Energy

The house has energy delivered either by connection to a mains network or in bulk. In either case, it is possible to express the energy content of the fuel in common units such as kWh. Metered supplies of electricity and gas are sold to the consumer in kWh. Fuels supplied in bulk are sold by weight or volume, but the units used for sale can readily be converted to kWh by using the calorific value of the fuel. For example, a litre of heating oil has an energy content of 10.35 kWh. This – the energy content of fuel delivered - is known as **delivered energy.**

It should be apparent, however, that not all forms of delivered energy are equally useful. Electrical energy can be converted to heat with 100% efficiency and can operate motors, lights and electronic circuits. But that versatility comes at price: electricity has been generated from fuel consumed at power stations with an average efficiency of around 40%. The energy at the power station used to provide a household with 1 kWh of delivered electricity is therefore considerably greater at around 2.5 kWh. This is known as **primary energy**, and takes account of the energy overhead required for generation and distribution. There are also energy overheads associated with the production, refining and distribution of fuels, although these are much smaller than for electricity, typically around 5%.

The distinction between delivered and primary energy is important when considering energy running cost and environmental impact, both of which are more closely related to primary than delivered energy. Electricity is clearly a premium source of energy, which is vastly more versatile at the point of use than other forms, but that is reflected in both its cost and the overall environmental impact of fuel used in its production. In 1990, UK electricity generation relied on coal for 67% of its energy input. By 1998 that had fallen to just 33%, while the proportion of natural gas used had risen from less than 1% to 33%. Further displacement of coal by gas is expected, leading to improved power station efficiency and reduced CO_2 emissions per unit of delivered electricity.

Nevertheless, electricity remains an expensive means of heating, with a cost per kWh about 5 times that of natural gas at on-peak rates and about twice at off-peak rates. Carbon dioxide emissions per unit of delivered electricity also remain high, at about 2.5 times those for gas. This does not mean that electricity should never be used for heating, but both cost and environmental considerations should confine it to cases where there is low demand; i.e, in small properties with high standards of insulation, good control, and where a large proportion of consumption can be at off-peak rates.

4.4 Why Energy Efficiency is Important

Energy efficiency produces benefits for individual householders and for the environment.

For households, the benefits are lower fuel bills and more comfortable conditions. A well insulated house needs less heat to bring it up to a comfortable temperature and cools down more slowly when the heating system is turned off. An efficient, well controlled heating system uses less fuel to produce a given amount of heat. Both combine to reduce the total amount of fuel needed and hence the cost. Affordable heating is of particular importance in the social housing sector, which caters for households with low incomes. Consequently, contractors working for housing associations and local authorities need to pay particular attention to energy efficiency.

The environmental benefits of energy efficiency were discussed in section 4.2 above. Energy efficiency contributes to reduced environmental impact through the use of less fuel. It is also important to take account of the difference in carbon emissions between fuels, particularly the high emissions associated with electricity use. While replacing a gas boiler by electric heating might appear advantageous in reducing the requirement for delivered energy, it would cause a substantial increase in environmental impact as well as running costs. Table 4.1 gives CO_2 emissions per unit of delivered energy for electricity and heating fuels in the UK.

Fuel	CO_2 emissions in kg/kWh
Gas (mains)	0.19
LPG	0.25
Heating oil	0.27
Solid fuels	0.29 to 0.39
Electricity (1997)	0.51

TABLE 4.1: CO_2 EMISSION FACTORS FOR DELIVERED ENERGY IN THE UK

4.5 The Standard Assessment Procedure (SAP) and Heat Energy Rating

A home energy rating is a measure of the energy efficiency of a dwelling. SAP is the UK Government's standard methodology for home energy rating, and the Heat Energy Rating is the equivalent scheme in the Republic of Ireland. These have to be applied to all new housing. SAP and HER are based on running costs for space- and water-heating and depend on the form of the building, its thermal insulation, which fuel is used and the performance of the heating system. Ratings are expressed on a range of 1 to 100, the higher the better. SAP ratings allow comparisons of energy efficiency to be made and can show the likely effect of improvements to a dwelling in terms of energy use. Using energy ratings, designers, developers, house-builders, and home owners can take energy efficiency factors into consideration both for new dwellings and when refurbishing existing ones. Energy ratings can be used at the design stage as a guide to energy efficiency and the reduction of future fuel bills. The SAP procedure also generates a Carbon Index. This is quoted on a scale of 0.0 to 10.0 and represents the CO_2 emissions associated with space and water heating adjusted for floor area, so that it is essentially independent of dwelling size. Higher numbers represent better performance, ie. lower CO_2 emissions.

The heating designer has an important opportunity to influence the SAP or HER rating through the choice of a boiler with high efficiency, the choice of fuel and the specification of good controls. SEDBUK (see Section 4.7 below) was specifically designed to provide values for boiler efficiency use in SAP calculations, and has been used in SAP assessments since July 1999.

4.6   Boiler Efficiency

The efficiency of the boiler is the main factor affecting the energy efficiency of gas- and oil-fired wet central heating systems. Minimum standards of efficiency for most types of boiler are imposed by law, which in the UK is the *Boiler (Efficiency) Regulations 1993* (UK legislation implementing the European Union Boiler Efficiency Directive) and in the Republic of Ireland the European Communities (Efficiency Requirements for Hot Water Boilers fired with liquid and Gaseous Fuels) Regulations 1994.

Boiler efficiency depends both on the design of the boiler and conditions under which it operates. Boiler design features affecting efficiency include:

- size (surface area) of heat exchanger
- water content of the heat exchanger;
- the method of ignition, especially whether or not it relies on a permanent pilot flame;
- the type of burner control (on/off, gas modulating or gas/air modulating);
- whether or not the boiler is designed to operate in condensing mode; and
- flue shape and length.

Operating conditions affecting boiler efficiency include:

- the size (power rating) of the boiler in relation to the design heat load and radiator sizes;
- the heating system controls; and
- flow and return water temperatures.

All three are at least in part within the control of the designer, while installation and commissioning are important to the realisation of the designer's intentions. Regular servicing and maintenance are also necessary to ensure that efficiency is sustained, particularly for oil fired boilers.

The principal factor under the system designer's control is the selection of the boiler itself. Information on the efficiency of gas and oil boilers in the UK can be obtained from the boiler efficiency database, which is accessible via the Internet at **www.boilers.org.uk** (see section

4.7 below). The reader is also referred to Good Practice Guide 284 *Domestic central heating and hot water: systems with gas and oil-fired boilers*, published by the UK Government's Energy Efficiency Best Practice Programme.

4.7 SEDBUK

SEDBUK is an acronym for 'Seasonal Efficiency of a Domestic Boiler in the UK'. The method used in SEDBUK was developed under the UK Government's Energy Efficiency Best Practice Programme with the co-operation of boiler manufacturers, and provides a basis for fair comparison of different models.

SEDBUK is the average annual efficiency achieved in typical domestic conditions, making reasonable assumptions about pattern of usage, climate, control, and other influences. It is calculated from the results of standard laboratory tests together with other important factors such as boiler type, ignition arrangement, internal store size, fuel used, and knowledge of the UK climate and typical domestic usage patterns. For estimating annual fuel costs SEDBUK is a better guide than laboratory test results alone. It can be applied to most gas and oil domestic boilers for which data is available from tests conducted to the relevant European standards. The SEDBUK method is used in SAP.

As a simple guide to efficiency, a scheme has been created with SEDBUK efficiency bands assigned to boilers on an "A" to "G" scale. (see Fig 4.1 below). The band is shown in the database and may be used on product literature and labels, though there is no requirement for manufacturers to do so. The scheme is temporary as it will be withdrawn when a European directive on boiler energy labelling is introduced.

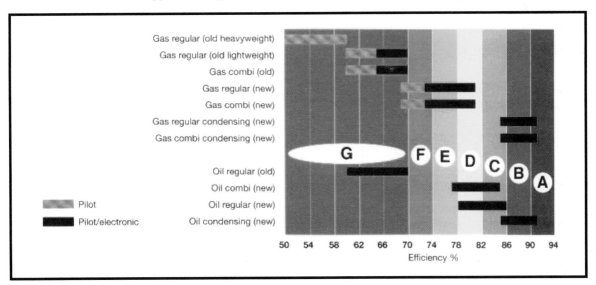

FIG 4.1 TYPICAL SEDBUK RANGES FOR BOILER TYPES

4.8 Condensing Boilers

The heat exchanger in a condensing boiler is designed to extract maximum heat from the flue gases. To do so, it reduces the temperature of the flue gases to below the dew point of the flue gases, which causes water vapour to condense on the surfaces of the heat exchanger, a situation that is deliberately avoided in other boilers. The presence of condensation in large quantities requires that the heat exchanger be made of corrosion-resistant materials and that a drain is provided for the condensate.

15

Condensing boilers are significantly more efficient, as non-condensing boilers have to be designed to operate with flue gas temperatures high enough to avoid the accumulation of condensate that would cause corrosion. Even the least efficient condensing gas boiler is about 3% more efficient than the best non-condensing boiler, and the difference is typically about 13%. Condensing boilers are most efficient when operating with low return water temperatures, which induce high levels of condensation. However, they are significantly more efficient than other boilers when operated under normal conditions found in a domestic installation, even though not condensing all the time. Although it is possible to increase the proportion of time boilers operate in condensing mode by installing larger radiators and using lower flow and return temperature, it is neither necessary nor to be recommended; field trials have shown it to be not cost-effective.

From the installer's point of view, there are two particular considerations to be taken into account when specifying condensing boilers: the provision of a drain for the condensate and the acceptability of 'pluming'– the production of a visible cloud of water droplets - from the flue. The condensate drain does not normally cause a problem, although care must be taken to ensure that it can be kept clear. Pluming can be a real problem, however, when the flue discharges into an area close to neighbouring property. Pluming may be perceived as much less acceptable than the less visible and more buoyant combustion products from a non-condensing boiler. Condensing boilers are thought by some installers to be more difficult to maintain and less reliable but there is no reason why a condensing boiler should be different from any other modern boiler in these respects. There is little difference in complexity and the only additional maintenance task is to ensure that the condensate drain is kept clear.

For gas installations, condensing boilers should be specified unless the additional costs outweigh the benefits or where there are serious difficulties with terminal siting, pluming or connection to a drain. For oil installations, condensing boilers have less of an advantage over non-condensing types, which are generally more efficient than their gas counterparts.

4.9   Cylinders

Hot water storage cylinders affect energy efficiency for two main reasons. Firstly, they should be well insulated, as heat lost to the surroundings cannot contribute usefully to space heating requirements when no heat is required in summer and may contribute to uncomfortably high temperatures. Of course insulation is especially important if the cylinder is located in an unheated space. Secondly, cylinder heat exchangers should have sufficient capacity to provide rapid warm-up; poor heat exchanger performance causes the boiler to be on for long periods at low loads. Apart from providing poor service to the household, this reduces boiler efficiency and increases heat losses from the primary circuit.

As a minimum, the designer should always specify hot water cylinders that comply with BS 1566 or BS3198. 'High performance' cylinders, which have fast recovery heat exchangers and are usually also better insulated, are recommended. However, 'medium duty' cylinders should be avoided as they are usually both badly insulated and have poor heat exchanger performance.

4.10 Controls

The output required from a heating system varies considerably, particularly in response to external temperature. Controls are needed to ensure that the system provides the appropriate output for all conditions, including those where little or no additional heat is required. Controls contribute significantly to the efficient operation of a heating system, by allowing the desired temperatures to be achieved in each room at the times required. The selection of appropriate controls also plays a key part in the overall running costs of a heating system.

For example, upgrading controls on older heating systems can save up to 15% on energy bills. The recommended minimum set of controls is given in Good Practice Guide 302 *Controls for domestic heating and hot water systems.* See also General Information Leaflet 83 *Domestic boiler anti-cycling controls* – an evaluation concerning claims made for boiler anti-cycling devices.

Section 18 of this Guide describes the operation of the principal types of control and specifies appropriate packages of controls for different types of system.

4.11 Specifying efficient systems

To help purchasers to specify efficient heating, a set of simple standards has been prepared, known as "CHeSS" (Central Heating Systems Specifications). It was first published in February 2001 and gives recommendations for current good practice and best practice, for the energy efficiency of domestic wet central heating systems. It explains to purchasers and suppliers how the efficiency-critical components should be specified, using four simple names for reference:

> **CHeSS HR3 (2002)**: regular boiler and hot water store system – *basic*
>
> **CHeSS HC3 (2002)**: combination boiler or CPSU system – *basic*
>
> **CHeSS HR4 (2002)**: regular boiler and hot water store system – *best practice*
>
> **CHeSS HC4 (2002)**: combination boiler or CPSU system – *best practice*

Basic systems are sufficient to comply with Building Regulations 2000 Part L1 (Conservation of fuel and power in dwellings) which came into effect in England and Wales in April 2002, and Building Standards (Scotland) Regulations Part J which came into effect in March 2002. Part L1 now applies to replacement heating systems in existing housing, as well as new ones.

CHeSS was produced in response to a request from the Heating Strategy Group of the Energy Efficiency Partnership for Homes, which recognised that one of the difficulties facing the domestic heating installation industry was a lack of common standards and understanding of what should be done to improve energy efficiency.

CHeSS has become widely used by purchasers and installers, especially in government policy initiatives and installation schemes for more efficient domestic heating. Details may be obtained free from the Housing Helpline on 01923-664258, reference GIL 59.

5.0 HEAT LOSSES AND U-VALUES

5.1 Basic Principles

Heat flows by conduction through materials, by convection in fluids and by radiation. All three of those mechanisms are relevant to domestic heating system design. The designer's task is first to estimate the heat the system must provide to maintain the dwelling at the required indoor temperature under the most demanding conditions specified. Calculations are undertaken on a room-by-room basis to allow the required heat output for each room to be assessed and heat emitters to be sized. The overall heat load to be provided by the boiler can then be calculated and the boiler sized accordingly.

5.2 Calculation of Heat Loss

There are two significant mechanisms to consider in calculating the heat lost from a house:

- heat is conducted through the fabric of the building – its walls, roof, ground floor, windows and doors. This is sometimes referred to as 'fabric heat loss'.
- heat is lost when warm air leaves the house and cold incoming air must be warmed to replace that heat. This is generally known as 'ventilation heat loss'.

Both types of heat loss need to be calculated and taken into account in heating system design.

5.3 Calculation of Fabric Heat Loss

The rate at which heat is lost by conduction through a building element depends on the temperature difference across the element, its area, and its propensity to conduct heat. The last of those factors depends on the thermal conductivity of the materials from which the element is constructed and the thickness of layers of those materials. For example, a solid brick wall conducts heat faster than a wall of the same thickness made of insulating concrete blocks, whilst a thin wall conducts heat faster than a thick one.

The rate at which a building element conducts heat is given by its 'U-value', which is the number of Watts that will flow though an area of one square metre when subjected to a temperature difference of 1 Kelvin, K. (One K is the same as a 1 degree C temperature difference).[2] For example, a standard cavity wall with no insulation has a U-value of about 1.5 W/ (m^2K). To work out the rate at which heat is lost by the whole wall per degree of temperature difference, multiply the U-value by the wall area, giving a result in W/K. This can be done for each heat-losing surface of the building or room and the results added. Finally the design temperature difference between indoors and outdoors can be taken into account by multiplying the total surface heat losses at a 1°C difference by the design temperature difference. This gives the design structural building 'element' heat loss in Watts.

---

[2] The kelvin (K) is the international standard unit of thermodynamic temperature and is used to express temperature difference as well as 'absolute' temperature (T). The degree Celsius, commonly used to express room temperature, is defined as t°C = T- 273.15, where T is in kelvins.

Rate of heat loss (Watts) = A.U. ($T_{in} - T_{out}$),

where

A is the area of the building element in m^2,
U is its U-value in $W/(m^2K)$
T_{in} is the indoor temperature in °C, and
T_{out} is the outdoor temperature in °C

The rate of fabric heat loss for the whole house may be calculated by adding the results thus obtained for each element.

5.4   Ventilation Heat Loss

Ventilation heat loss depends upon the rate at which air enters and leaves the building, the heat capacity of the air itself and the temperature difference between indoors and outdoors. The heat capacity of air is approximately constant under the conditions encountered in a house so the other two factors determine the overall result. The quantity of air passing through the building depends upon the volume of the building and the air change rate, which is usually expressed in air change per hour (ach). The ventilation heat loss rate of a room or building may be calculated by the formula:

Rate of heat loss = 0.33 V.N   (W/K),

where

V is volume of the room in m^3, and
N is the number of air changes per hour.

The factor 0.33 is the product of the specific heat and density of air under typical conditions. Multiply the result so obtained by the temperature difference between indoors and outdoors to get the heat loss in Watts.

5.5   Calculation of U-Values

U-values can mostly be obtained by reference to the tables given in Section 6 of this Guide. However, when the U-value for a particular construction element is not available, it can be calculated from the thickness and thermal conductivity of the layers in the construction.

For each layer, the thermal resistance R_i (m^2K/W) may be calculated by dividing its thickness in metres (m) by its thermal conductivity (W/m/K). The thermal conductivity of the building material can be obtained from the manufacturer or from tables such as those in CIBSE Guide A and Building Regulations. The thermal resistances of air gaps and surfaces should also be taken into account using the values given in Table 5.1 below.

Type of surface/air gap	Thermal resistance (m^2K/W)
Outside surface of exterior wall	0.06
Inside surface of wall	0.12
Air gap (cavity)	0.18

TABLE 5.1

The total thermal resistance of the element is calculated by adding up the thermal resistances of its layers:

$$R = R_{si} + R_1 + R_2 \ldots + R_a + R_{so}, \quad \text{where}$$

R_{si} = internal surface resistance
$R_1, R_2, .$ = thermal resistances of the layers
R_a = airspace resistance
R_{so} = outside surface resistance

The U-value is simply the reciprocal of the thermal resistance:

$$U = 1/R$$

5.6   Example Calculation

The following example shows a U-value calculation for the external wall construction shown in Figure 5.1. The outside surface is on the left.

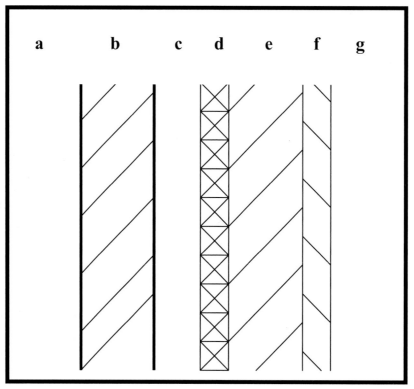

Fig. 5.1

Layer	Thermal Conductivity (W/mK)	Thermal Resistance (m^2K/W)
a External surface resistance		0.060
b 102.5mm facing brick	0.84 (exposed)	0.122
c 50mm airspace		0.180
d 25mm insulation	0.04	0.625
e 100mm thermal block	0.17 (protected)	0.588
f 13mm plaster	0.16	0.081
g inside surface resistance		0.120

TABLE 5.2

Table 5.2 shows the properties of the layers contributing to the thermal resistance of the wall. The calculation below shows the thermal resistance of each layer and for all layers together.

CALCULATION		Resistances R m^2K/W
a External surface	=	0.060
b Brick 0.1025/0.84	=	0.122
c Airspace	=	0.180
d Insulation 0.025/0.04	=	0.625
e Block 0.1/0.17	=	0.588
f Plaster 0.013/0.16	=	0.081
g Inside surface	=	0.120
Total Resistance R	=	1.776

U-value of construction $= 1/1.776 =$ $0.56W/m^2K$

5.7 Complex Structures

The calculation of U-values for complicated structures is beyond the scope of this Design Guide, and in such cases reference should be made to Section A3 of the CIBSE Guide where the subject is fully covered. The 'proportional area method' is currently recommended by building regulations for dealing with particular encountered constructions. Proposals for amending the energy efficiency provisions in building regulations, which are currently under consultation, recommend the 'combined method' specified in BS EN ISO 13370 and CIBSE Guide Section A3 (1999 edition).

5.8 Ground Floor U-Values

The calculation of U-values for ground floors is complex and cannot be achieved in the same way as for other structural components, since the thermal transmission varies according to the shape of the room and the proportion of exposed edge to the total floor area. Building regulations give a formula for calculating the U value of an uninsulated floor (U_0) based on the ratio of its exposed perimeter to its area:

$$U_0 = 0.05 + 1.65 (P/A) - 0.6(P/A)^2,$$

where P is the length of exposed perimeter (m) and

A is the floor area (m^2).

This formula applies to all types of floor construction including slab-on-ground and suspended floors. Unheated spaces outside the insulated fabric, such as attached garages or porches, should be treated as though they are not present when determining P and A.

5.9   Building Regulations

Building Regulations require good standards of insulation and the provision of certain types of heating control for new buildings and buildings undergoing 'material alterations and change of use'. The requirements have undergone successive revisions and offer a range of different methods of achieving compliance. These include U-values for individual building elements, see **Figure 5.2** below, target average U-values for the whole building and calculations based on the Standard Assessment Procedure (in the United Kingdom) or the Heat Energy Rating (in the Republic of Ireland). The reader is referred to the current version of the relevant Building Regulations for a detailed description of the requirements. See also page 110.

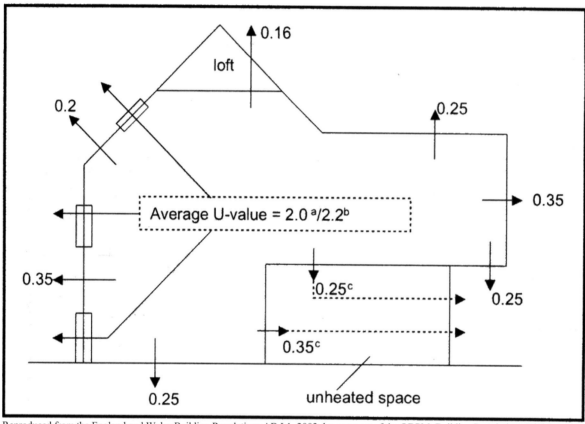

Reproduced from the England and Wales Building Regulations AD L1 2002, by courtesy of the ODPM, Building Regulations Division.

FIG 5.2 U-values for individual building elements for use with the Elemental Method of heat loss calculations in Building Regulations (See also **Table 6.17** on page 33)

Notes to **Figure 5.2**
a   if windows have wood or PVC frames
b   if windows have metal frames
c   includes the effect of the unheated space, as follows

Party walls, separating two dwellings or other premises that can reasonably be assumed to be heated to the same temperature, are assumed not to need thermal insulation.

6.0 U-VALUE TABLES

EXTERNAL WALLS		U-value W/m²K	
Solid brick wall, dense plaster			
	Brick 102 mm, plaster	2.97	
	Brick 228 mm, plaster	2.11	
	Brick 343 mm, plaster	1.64	
Solid stone wall, unplastered			
	Stone 305 mm (12in)	2.78	
	Stone 457 mm (18in)	2.23	
	Stone 610 mm (24 in)	1.68	
Solid concrete wall, dense plaster			
	Concrete 102mm, plaster	3.51	
	Concrete 152mm, plaster	3.12	
	Concrete 204mm, plaster	2.80	
	Concrete 254 mm, plaster	2.54	
Cavity wall, (Open cavity or mineral wool slab), lightweight plaster		**Open Cavity**	**Mineral Wool Slab 50 mm**
	Brick 102mm, brick 102mm, 13mm plaster	1.37	0.56
	Brick 102m, brick 102mm, 12.5mm plasterboard on dabs	1.21	0.53
Cavity wall, aerated block inner leaf, lightweight plaster		**Inner leaf thickness**	
		100mm	**125mm**
	Brick 102mm, cavity, standard aerated block (k=0.17), 13mm plaster	0.87	0.77
	Brick 102mm, cavity, standard aerated block (k=0.17), 12.5mm plasterboard on dabs	0.80	0.72
	Brick 102mm, mineral wool slab in cavity 50mm, standard aerated block (k=0.17), 13mm plaster	0.45	0.42
	Brick 102mm, mineral wool slab in cavity 50mm, standard aerated block (k=0.17), 12.5mm plasterboard on dabs	0.43	0.41

TABLE 6.1

EXTERNAL WALLS		U-value W/m^{2}K	
Cavity wall, aerated block inner leaf, lightweight plaster or plasterboard		**Inner leaf thickness**	
		100mm	**125mm**
	Brick 102mm, cavity, high performance aerated block (k=0.11), 13mm plaster	0.68	0.59
	Brick 102mm, cavity, high performance aerated block (k=0.11), 12.5mm plasterboard on dabs	0.64	0.56
	Brick 102mm, mineral wool slab in cavity 50mm, high performance aerated block (k=0.11), 13mm plaster	0.39	0.36
	Brick 102mm, mineral wool slab in cavity 50mm, high performance aerated block(k=0.11), 12.5mm plasterboard on dabs	0.38	0.35
Rendered Cavity wall, (Open cavity or mineral wool slab), lightweight plaster		**Open cavity**	**Mineral wool slab**
	Render 19mm, brick 102mm, brick 102mm, 13mm plaster	1.25	0.54
	Render 19mm, brick 102mm, brick 102mm, 12.5mm plasterboard on dabs	1.11	0.51
Rendered cavity wall, aerated block inner leaf, lightweight plaster or plasterboard		**Inner leaf thickness**	
		100mm	**125mm**
	Render 19mm, brick 102mm, cavity, standard aerated block, 13mm plaster	0.82	0.73
	Render 19mm, brick 102.5mm, mineral wool slab in cavity 50mm, standard aerated block, 13mm plaster	0.44	0.41
	Render 19mm, standard aerated block 100mm, cavity, standard aerated block, 13mm plaster	0.61	0.56
Rendered cavity wall, inner aerated block, lightweight plaster		**Inner leaf thickness**	
		100mm	**125mm**
	Render 19mm, standard aerated block 100mm mineral wool slab in cavity 50mm, std. Aerated block, 13mm plaster	0.37	0.35

TABLE 6.2

EXTERNAL WALLS	U-value W/m²K	
Rendered cavity wall, inner aerated block, lightweight plaster	**Inner leaf thickness**	
	100mm	125mm
Render 19mm, standard aerated block 100mm, cavity, high performance aerated block (k=0.11), 13mm plaster	0.51	0.45
Render 19mm, standard aerated block 100mm, mineral wool slab in cavity 50mm, high performance aerated block (k=0.11), 13mm plaster	0.33	0.31
Rendered Solid Wall		
Render 19mm, high performance aerated block (k=0.11) 215mm, 13mm plaster	0.44	
Tile clad cavity wall, (Open cavity or mineral wool slab), lightweight plaster	**Inner block thickness**	
	100mm	125mm
Tiles, airspace, standard aerated block, 13mm plaster	0.58	0.53
Tiles, airspace, standard aerated block 100mm, mineral wool slab in cavity 50mm, standard aerated block, 13mm plaster	0.36	0.34
Tiles, airspace, standard aerated block 100mm, cavity, high performance aerated block (k=0.11), 13mm plaster	0.49	0.44
Tile clad cavity wall,, (Open cavity or mineral wool slab), lightweight plaster	**Inner block thickness**	
	100mm	125mm
Tiles, airspace, standard aerated block 100mm, mineral wool slab in cavity 50mm, high performance aerated block (k=0.11), 13mm plaster	0.32	0.30
Tile Clad Solid Wall		
Tiles, airspace, high performance aerated block 215mm, 13mm plaster	0.43	
Timber Clad Cavity Wall		
Shiplap boards, airspace, standard aerated block 100mm, cavity, standard aerated block, 13mm plaster	0.53	0.49

TABLE 6.3

EXTERNAL WALLS		U-value W/m²K	
Timber Clad Cavity Wall			
	Shiplap boards, airspace, standard aerated block 100mm, mineral wool slab in cavity 50mm, standard aerated block, 13mm plaster	0.34	0.32
	Shiplap boards, airspace, standard aerated block 100mm, cavity, high performance aerated block, 13mm plaster	0.45	0.41
	Shiplap boards, airspace, standard aerated block 100mm, mineral wool slab in cavity 50mm, high performance block, 13mm plaster	0.31	0.29

Timber frame wall with cladding, membrane, plywood, studding, vapour membrane, plasterboard		**Insulation thickness**		
		60mm	**80mm**	**100mm**
	Brick 102.5mm, cavity, membrane, plywood 10mm, studding 100mm, with infill insulation, vapour membrane, plasterboard 12.5mm	0.43	0.36	0.32
	Tiles, airspace, membrane, plywood 10mm. Studding 100mm, with infill insulation, vapour membrane, plasterboard 12.5mm	0.47	0.38	0.34
	Shiplap boards, airspace, membrane, plywood 10mm, studding 100mm with infill insulation, vapour membrane, plasterboard 12.5mm	0.44	0.36	0.32

TABLE 6.4

INTERNAL WALLS		U-value W/m²K
	Plasterboard 12.5mm, studding 75mm, plasterboard 12.5mm	1.72
	Plaster 13mm, block 10mm, cavity, block 100mm, plaster 13mm	1.02
	Plaster 13mm, brick 102.5mm, plaster 13mm	1.76

TABLE 6.5

INTERNAL WALLS	U-value W/m^{2}K
Plaster 13mm, brick 215mm, plaster 13mm	1.33
Plaster, breeze block 100mm, plaster	1.58
Plaster 13mm, standard aerated block 100mm, plaster 13mm	1.66
Plaster 13mm, standard aerated block 125mm, plaster 13mm	1.53

TABLE 6.6

ROOFS	U-value W/m^{2}K				
Flat roof, timber construction, insulation and plasterboard	Insulation thickness (mm)				
	Nil	50	100	200	300
Chippings, 3 layers of felt, boarding, air space, insulation, 9.5 mm plasterboard	1.69	0.53	0.32	0.17	0.12
30° Pitched roof with tiles					
Slates or tiles, sarking felt, ventilated air space, insulation between joists, 9.5 mm plasterboard	2.51	0.60	0.34	0.18	0.12
Slates or tiles, ventilated air space, insulation between joists, 9.5 mm plasterboard	3.13	0.62	0.35	0.18	0.12
Slates or tiles, sarking felt, air space, insulation between rafters, 9.5 mm plasterboard	2.51	0.60	0.34	0.18	0.12

TABLE 6.7

WINDOWS AND DOORS	
The U-values listed below apply to the whole window including the frame and assume a standard gap between panes of 12mm	
Windows with wood or PVC-U frames	**U-value W/m²K**
Single	4.8
Double	2.8
Double, low-E glass	2.1
Double, low-E glass, argon filled	1.9
Triple	2.1
Triple, low-E glass	1.6
Triple, low-E glass, argon filled	1.5
Windows with metal frames	
Single	5.7
Double	3.4
Double, low-E glass	2.6
Double, low-E glass, argon filled	2.4
Triple	2.6
Triple, low-E glass	2.0
Triple, low-E glass, argon filled	1.9
Solid wooden door	3.0

TABLE 6.8

SOLID GROUND FLOORS IN CONTACT WITH EARTH					
Solid ground floor with TWO ADJACENT EDGES EXPOSED insulation slabs laid below screed with 25mm thick edge insulation. Floor finished with thermoplastic tiles or similar. Thermal conductivity of insulation = 0.04 W/mK					
Length of Exposed Wall a+b (m)	U-values, W/m²K for insulation thickness mm:-				
	Nil	25	50	75	100
5	1.02	0.58	0.41	0.31	0.26
6	0.90	0.54	0.39	0.30	0.25
7	0.82	0.51	0.37	0.29	0.24
8	0.76	0.49	0.36	0.28	0.23
9 - 10	0.70	0.46	0.34	0.27	0.23
10 - 12	0.60	0.41	0.32	0.26	0.22
12 - 14	0.52	0.38	0.29	0.24	0.21
14 - 17	0.45	0.34	0.27	0.23	0.19
17 - 20	0.39	0.30	0.25	0.21	0.18
Example room size = 6.5 x 5.0m = 11.5m exposed wall. U-value with 50mm insulation = 0.32 W/m²K					

TABLE 6.9

Solid ground floor with THREE EDGES EXPOSED, the shortest being the single exposed edge. (Use this table for square rooms). Insulation slabs laid below screed with 25mm edge insulation. Floor finish as above. Thermal conductivity of insulation = 0.04 W/mK	

SHORT Length a(m)	LONG Length b(m)	U-values Wm²K for insulation thickness mm:-				
		Nil	25	50	75	100
3	3 - 4	1.15	0.62	0.43	0.32	0.26
3	4 - 6	1.03	0.58	0.41	0.31	0.26
3	6 - 8	1.00	0.57	0.40	0.31	0.25
3	8 - 10	0.96	0.56	0.40	0.31	0.25
4	4 - 6	0.95	0.56	0.40	0.31	0.25
4	6 - 10	0.85	0.52	0.38	0.29	0.24
5	5 - 7	0.81	0.51	0.37	0.29	0.24
5	7 - 10	0.74	0.48	0.35	0.28	0.23
6	6 - 8	0.71	0.46	0.35	0.28	0.23
6	8 - 10	0.65	0.44	0.33	0.27	0.22

Example: Room = 5.0 x 6.5m U-value with 50mm insulation = 0.37 W/m²K

Solid ground floor with THREE EDGES EXPOSED, the longest being the single exposed edge. Insulation as previously specified	

SHORT Length a(m)	LONG Length b(m)	U-values W/m²K for insulation thickness mm				
		Nil	25	50	75	100
3	3 - 5	1.05	0.59	0.41	0.32	0.26
3	5 - 7	0.90	0.54	0.39	0.30	0.25
3	7 - 9	0.85	0.52	0.38	0.29	0.24
3	9 - 10	0.77	0.49	0.36	0.28	0.24
4	4 - 6	0.95	0.56	0.40	0.31	0.25
4	6 - 8	0.87	0.53	0.38	0.30	0.24
4	8 - 10	0.76	0.49	0.36	0.28	0.24
5	5 - 7	0.83	0.51	0.37	0.29	0.24
5	7 - 9	0.77	0.49	0.36	0.28	0.24
5	9 - 10	0.68	0.45	0.34	0.27	0.23
6	6 - 8	0.75	0.48	0.36	0.28	0.23
6	6 - 10	0.70	0.46	0.34	0.27	0.23

Solid ground floor with TWO OPPOSITE EDGES EXPOSED Insulation as previously specified	

DISTANCE Between Edges a(m)	U-values, W/m²K for insulation thickness mm:-				
	Nil	25	50	75	100
2	1.15	0.62	0.43	0.32	0.26
3	0.90	0.54	0.39	0.30	0.25
4	0.73	0.47	0.35	0.28	0.23
4 - 6	0.62	0.43	0.32	0.26	0.22
6 - 8	0.55	0.39	0.30	0.25	0.21
8 - 10	0.44	0.33	0.27	0.22	0.19

TABLE 6.10

Solid ground floor with ONE EDGE EXPOSED Insulation as previously specified					

DEPTH of Room a(m)	U-values, W/m²K for insulation thickness mm:-				
	Nil	25	50	75	100
1.5	0.90	0.54	0.39	0.30	0.25
2	0.73	0.47	0.35	0.28	0.23
3	0.55	0.39	0.30	0.25	0.21
3 - 5	0.45	0.34	0.27	0.23	0.19
5 - 7	0.38	0.30	0.24	0.21	0.18
7 - 10	0.28	0.23	0.20	0.17	0.15

TABLE 6.11

SUSPENDED GROUND FLOORS

Suspended ground floor with TWO ADJACENT EDGES EX-
POSED Insulation slabs laid between joists on polypropylene
net and covered with timber boarding.
Thermal conductivity of insulation = 0.04 W/mK

Length of Exposed Wall a + b (m)	U-values W/m²K for insulation thickness mm::-				
	Nil	25	50	75	100
5	1.05	0.59	0.41	0.32	0.26
6	0.93	0.55	0.39	0.30	0.25
7	0.86	0.53	0.38	0.30	0.24
8	0.79	0.50	0.37	0.29	0.24
9 - 10	0.75	0.48	0.36	0.28	0.23
10 - 12	0.65	0.44	0.33	0.27	0.22
12 - 14	0.58	0.41	0.31	0.25	0.21
14 - 17	0.71	0.37	0.29	0.24	0.20
17 - 20	0.43	0.33	0.26	0.22	0.19

Example: Room size = 6.5 x 5.0m = 11.5m exposed wall.
U-value with 50mm insulation = 0.33 W/m²K

TABLE 6.12

SUSPENDED GROUND FLOORS

Suspended ground floor with THREE EDGES EXPOSED, the shortest being the single exposed edge. (Use this table for square rooms). Insulation slabs laid between joists on polypropylene net and covered with timber boarding. Thermal conductivity of insulation = 0.04 W/mK

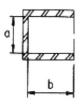

SHORT Length a(m)	LONG Length b(m)	U-values Wm²K for insulation thickness mm:-				
		Nil	25	50	75	100
3	3 - 4	1.15	0.62	0.43	0.32	0.26
3	4 - 6	1.03	0.58	0.41	0.31	0.26
3	6 - 8	1.00	0.57	0.40	0.31	0.25
3	8 - 10	0.99	0.56	0.40	0.31	0.25
4	4 - 6	0.95	0.56	0.40	0.31	0.25
4	6 - 10	0.87	0.53	0.38	0.30	0.24
5	5 - 7	0.83	0.51	0.37	0.29	0.24
5	7 - 10	0.80	0.50	0.37	0.29	0.24
6	6 - 8	0.75	0.48	0.36	0.28	0.23
6	8 - 10	0.72	0.47	0.35	0.28	0.23

Example: Room = 5.0 x 6.5m U-value with 50mm insulation = 0.37 W/m²K

Suspended ground floor with THREE EDGES EXPOSED, the longest being the single exposed edge. (Use this table for square rooms). Insulation as previously specified

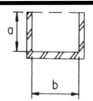

SHORT Length a(m)	LONG Length b(m)	U-values Wm²K for insulation thickness mm:-				
		Nil	25	50	75	100
3	3 - 5	1.00	0.57	0.40	0.31	0.25
3	5 - 7	0.85	0.52	0.38	0.29	0.24
3	7 - 9	0.80	0.50	0.37	0.29	0.24
3	9 - 10	0.77	0.49	0.36	0.28	0.24
4	4 - 6	0.85	0.52	0.38	0.29	0.24
4	6 - 8	0.79	0.50	0.37	0.29	0.24
4	8 - 10	0.73	0.47	0.35	0.28	0.23
5	5 - 7	0.77	0.49	0.36	0.28	0.24
5	7 - 9	0.72	0.47	0.35	0.28	0.23
5	9 - 10	0.66	0.44	0.33	0.27	0.22
6	6 - 8	0.69	0.46	0.34	0.27	0.23
6	6 - 10	0.67	0.45	0.34	0.27	0.23

Example: Room = 5.0 x 6.5m U-value with 50mm insulation = 0.37 W/m²K

TABLE 6.13

SUSPENDED GROUND FLOORS

Suspended ground floor with TWO OPPOSITE EDGES EX-POSED
Insulation as previously specified.

DISTANCE between edges a (m)	U-values W/m²K for insulation thickness mm:				
	Nil	25	50	75	100
2	1.10	0.61	0.42	0.32	0.26
3	0.95	0.56	0.40	0.31	0.25
4	0.83	0.51	0.37	0.29	0.23
4 - 6	0.74	0.48	0.35	0.26	0.23
6 - 8	0.67	0.45	0.34	0.27	0.23
8 - 10	0.55	0.39	0.30	0.25	0.21

Suspended ground floor with ONE EDGE EXPOSED
Insulation as previously specified.

DEPTH Of Room a (m)	U-values W/m²K for insulation thickness mm::-				
	Nil	25	50	75	100
1.5	1.10	0.61	0.42	0.32	0.26
2	0.83	0.51	0.37	0.29	0.24
3	0.67	0.45	0.34	0.27	0.23
3 - 5	0.56	0.40	0.31	0.25	0.21
5 - 7	0.48	0.35	0.28	0.23	0.20
7 - 10	0.38	0.30	0.24	0.21	0.19

TABLE 6.14

INTERNAL FLOORS EXPOSED UNDERSIDE

Timber floor with underside exposed to outside or unheated area. (heat flow-down)	Insulation thickness		
	nil	100mm	150mm
Boarding 19mm, airspace between joists, insulation, 6mm sheeting	1.75	0.33	0.23
Concrete slab with underside exposed to outside or unheated area. (heat flow-down)			
Screed 50mm, concrete slab 150mm, insulation between battens, 6mm sheeting	1.82	0.57	
Intermediate floors, boarding 19mm, airspace between joists, 9.5mm plasterboard			
Heat flow - upwards	1.73	0.32	
Heat flow - down	1.41	0.31	

TABLE 6.15

AIR	W/m^3K
The heat capacity by volume of air at 20°C, used to calculate heat loss due to air changes	0.33

TABLE 6.16

U-VALUES (W/M^2K) REQUIRED BY BUILDING REGULATIONS FOR NEW DWELLING CONSTRUCTION ELEMENTS – USING THE ELEMENTAL CALCULATION METHOD

Exposed Element	U-value
Pitched roof with insulation between rafters [1] [2]	0.2
Pitched roof with integral insulation	0.25
Pitched roof with insulation between joists	0.16
Flat roof [3]	0.25
Walls, including basement walls	0.35
Floors, including ground floors and basement floors	0.25
Windows, doors and rooflights [4] (area-weighted average), glazing in metal frames [5]	2.2
Windows, doors and rooflights [4] (area-weighted average), glazing in wood or PVC frames [5]	2.0

See page 22 for a graphical representation of above U-values.

Notes to Table:

1. Any part of a roof having a pitch of 70° or more can be considered as a wall.
2. For the sloping parts of a room-in-the-roof constructed as a material alteration, a U-value of 0.3 W/m^2K would be reasonable.
3. Roof of pitch not exceeding 10°
4. Rooflights include roof windows
5. The higher U-value for metal-framed windows allows for additional solar gain due to the greater glazed proportion.

Reproduced from the England and Wales Building Regulations AD L1 2002, by courtesy of the ODPM, Building Regulations Division

TABLE 6.17

7.0 VENTILATION IN LIVING SPACES

7.1 Ventilation Requirements

Ventilation is needed to provide enough fresh air to living spaces to restrict the build-up of moisture, pollutants and odours. Building regulations set requirements for ventilation in dwellings, which are usually met by the installation of extractor fans in kitchens and bathrooms, and by openable windows and trickle ventilators in other rooms. The heat loss arising from ventilation has already been dealt with in Section 5 above and it is clearly preferable to minimise ventilation when considering heating requirements. However, this should not be done to the extent that it harms air quality and the task of the heating system designer is to provide a system that is capable of coping with the total expected heat load.

7.2 Minimum Requirements for Ventilation

Building regulations also give guidance on how adequate ventilation may be provided in dwellings. It aims both to achieve rapid extraction of moisture from kitchens and bathrooms and to provide background ventilation in other rooms. Typical requirements are summarised in the table below. Refer to the relevant part of the current building regulations applying where the dwelling is located.

Room	Rapid ventilation	Background (area of opening)	Extract ventilation
Living rooms, dining rooms and bedrooms	opening 1/20 of floor area	8000 mm^2	Not required
Kitchen	opening window (no minimum size)	4000 mm^2	30 litres/s adjacent to hob or 60 litres/s elsewhere
Utility room	opening window (no minimum size)	4000 mm^2	30 litres/s
Bathroom (with or without WC)	opening window (no minimum size)	4000 mm^2	15 litres/s
Toilet (separate from bathroom)	opening 1/20 of floor area (not required if mechanical extract ventilation provided)	4000 mm^2	Capable of extracting at a rate of not less than 3 air changes an hour, which may be operated intermittently with 15 minutes overrun

TABLE 7.1

Passive stack ventilation may be used as an alternative to mechanical extract ventilation provided it is designed in accordance with BRE Information Paper 13/94 or with appropriate 3rd party certification, such as a BBA certificate.

Further guidance on ventilation may be found in BS 5250:1989 *Code of Practice: the control of Condensation in buildings*.

7.3 Fan Duty Selection

The possibility exists for the performance of any fan or cooker hood, even when used intermittently, to exceed the design air change rate of the room and thereby increase the amount of heat required to meet the design temperature. This, however, can usually be disregarded as the temperature gains from the cooking appliances or bathing water will offset the problem. Careful consideration should, however, be given to the selection of fan duties to ensure larger volumes of air than necessary are not extracted.

7.4 Whole House Mechanical Ventilation

The ventilation requirements of the Building Regulations may also be met through the provision of whole-house mechanical ventilation, following the relevant recommendations set out in BS 5720: 1989 *Code of Practice for mechanical ventilation and air conditioning of buildings.* This type of ventilation may include heat recovery, which typically reduces the ventilation heat load by more than 50%.

7.5 Combustion Air and Ventilation Requirements for Heating Appliances

Building regulations set requirements for ventilation relating to heating appliances; this subject is dealt with in Section 19 of this Guide.

8.0 HEAT LOSS CALCULATIONS

8.1   Temperature requirements

BS 5449 lists different design temperatures for different rooms. In practice, the temperatures required depend on the preferences of individual households and the temperatures actually achieved depend on the provision of suitable means of control. It is therefore recommended that a design temperature of 22°C be used for bathrooms and 21°C for all other rooms. Where higher temperatures are required, for example for the elderly or infirm, a design temperature of 23°C is recommended for all rooms. Using a single design temperature has the advantage that the complexity of calculating heat transfer between rooms is avoided and only losses through external surfaces need be considered.

The client's preferences should be taken into account. However, when the client suggests that lower temperatures are adequate, make clear the advantages of designing a system with the capacity to reach the higher temperatures normally expected, for example, if the house were to be sold. Also, explain the risk of condensation occurring in unheated rooms when the rest of the house is heated. Finally, explain how controls may be adjusted to provide lower temperatures where and when desired.

8.2   External Temperatures

An external design temperature of -3°C should normally be used when calculating heat losses on a room-by-room basis. This may be lowered to take account of more severe local conditions, such as found in parts of Scotland and Northern England.

8.3   Air Change Rates

Table 8.1 shows air change rates recommended for use in calculating design heat loads. They are chosen to reflect peak conditions, for example, when extractor fans are in use or windows are opened, rather than long term averages.

ROOM	Air changes per hour	ROOM	Air changes per hour
Lounge/Sitting Room	1.5	Games Room	1.5
Living Room	1.5	Bedroom	1.0
Dining Room	1.5	Bedroom with en-suite Bathroom	2.0**
Kitchen	2.0*		
Breakfast Room	1.5	Bedsitting Room	1.5
Kitchen/Breakfast Room	2.0*	Bedroom/Study	1.5
Hall	2.0	Landing	2.0
Cloakroom	2.0*	Bathroom	3.0*
Toilet	3.0*	Shower Room	3.0*
Utility Room	3.0*	Dressing Room	1.5
Study	1.5	Store Room	1.0*

TABLE 8.1 RECOMMENDED DESIGN AIR CHANGE RATES

* Where mechanical extract ventilation is installed in a room it is possible for the minimum fan duty to exceed the minimum air change rate. In such cases it is advisable to allow for the increased air change in the heat loss calculation for both the room and the connecting rooms from which the air will be drawn.

** Where a shower or bath is fitted into a bedroom or where an opening without door exists between the bedroom and the en-suite facility, then the air change rate of the bedroom should be increased accordingly to allow for the movement of air caused by the extract fan.

8.4   Rooms with Open Flues

Where appliances with open flues are installed in a room the air change rate should be increased to allow for the movement of air into the chimney. Table 8.2 shows the rates for rooms with open fire flues up to 40,000mm² (200mm x 200mm). Air change rates will approximately double when the open fire is in use. Very tall chimneys, such as found in a multi-storey house, produce very strong draught and a correspondingly high ventilation rate.

Room volume (m³)	Throat restrictor fitted to flue	Air changes per hour
Up to 40	NO	5
Up to 40	YES	3
Up to 70	NO	4
Up to 70	YES	2

TABLE 8.2: VENTILATION ARISING FROM CHIMNEYS AND FLUES

8.5   Building Exposure

When a building is located in an exposed position, such as on top of a hill, by a riverside, at the coast, or in any extreme open location, allowance should be made for increased heat losses. For a windy location, this can be taken into account by increasing ventilation rates. Increased elevation may be accounted for by reducing the external temperature by 0.5°C for each 160 metres (500 ft) above sea level.

Alternatively, a general addition to heat losses may be made to allow for an exposed location. A 10% addition is recommended as a rule of thumb but this should be based on local conditions and increased if the location is particularly exposed.

8.6   High Ceilings

Rooms with unusually high ceilings need additional heat to compensate for the stratification of warmer air at the higher level. The following additions to the basic heat losses are recommended.

ROOM HEIGHT (m)	4.5	5.5	6.5	7.5
ADDITION (%)	2.5	5.0	7.5	10.0

TABLE 8.3 EFFECT OF ROOM HEIGHT ON HEAT LOSS

8.7   Adjoining Properties

The heat loss calculations for rooms in flats, semi-detached and terraced houses should assume that the adjoining property is unheated, even when it is known that a heating system is installed. This will then ensure that the design temperatures will be achieved when the adjoining building is unoccupied. Section 9.5 of this Guide includes guidance on how this may be carried out.

8.8   Intermittent Heating

Where the heating system may not be used continuously, additional capacity will be required in both radiator and boiler outputs to enable room design temperatures to be achieved in a reasonable period of time.

In older properties the addition of 10% to the heat loss is usually sufficient, but in modern well insulated properties with smaller heat requirements, or where heating systems are to be used for very short periods, the addition to the heat loss should not be less than 20%.

Diversity of the total heating requirement should not be considered when determining boiler power unless it is positively known that specific parts of the system will not be used at the same time.

9.0 A WORKSHEET FOR HEAT LOSS CALCULATIONS

9.1 Heat Loss

Heat losses are calculated on a room-by-room basis so that the heat output required in each room can be estimated and the radiators sized accordingly. Heat loss is calculated according to the principles set out in Section 5. This may be conveniently done using worksheets, which provide a framework for ensuring that all heat losses are treated systematically. Blank calculation sheets may be found on the CD ROM version of this Guide[1] or may be purchased in pads from the organisations sponsoring this publication. They may also be taken from the blank copies in Appendix F.

Worksheet one - Heat Losses, may be used to make the necessary calculations for a room. The surface areas are calculated from measurements and U-values may be taken from the Tables in Section 5 of this Guide. The ventilation heat loss is calculated from the room volume, the ventilation rate in air changes per hour and the temperature difference, using the factor given for the heat capacity. The fabric heat loss for each external surface of the room is calculated by multiplying together its area, its U-value and the difference between indoor and outdoor design temperature. The total heat loss for the room is obtained by adding together the losses from the room surfaces and the ventilation.

9.2 Design Temperatures

Use the temperatures given in Section 8 unless special conditions apply. Heat transfer between rooms may be disregarded, as a result of using the same design temperature for all rooms.

9.3 Ventilation Rates

Use the ventilation rates given in Table 8.1, adjusted to take account of open flues and high ceilings as described in Section 8.

9.4 Windows, Doors & Roof Glazing

Subtract the U-value of the wall or roof in which the opening is located from the U-value given for the glazing so that the value remaining represents the extra heat loss over and above what would occur if the opening were not there. This method means that the area of openings need not be subtracted from the area of the wall or roof in which they are located.

---

[1] Due to be made available in 2004.

9.5 Party Walls

Section 8 above has advised that adjoining properties should be assumed to be unheated. However, the temperature in the adjoining property will typically be considerably above outside temperature, so the effective U-value of the party wall will be lower than its nominal value. As a rule of thumb, halve the U-value of the party wall to take account of the reduced loss.

9.6 A Worked Example

The heat loss calculation sheet shown on the next page has been completed for the kitchen/dining room of the two bedroom end-of-terrace house shown Figure 9.1. The calculated heat loss then provides the basis for estimating the size of radiator required for that room, which is dealt with in the next section.

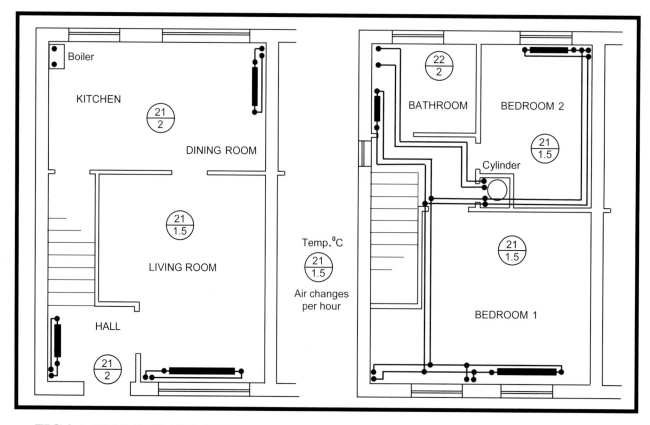

FIG 9.1 TWO BED END TERRACE HOUSE

DOMESTIC HEATING DESIGN GUIDE

WORKSHEET ONE – HEAT LOSSES

| ROOM | KITCHEN / DINING | | | | | Page | 2 of 6 |

	No. of air changes per hour	Room volume *Enter measurements*			Amount of air to be heated per hour *Calculate*	*Enter factor*	Heat loss/°C *Calculate* W/K
		Length	Width	Height			
	ach	m	m	m	m³/hour		
VENTILATION HEAT LOSS	2	4.9	2.7	2.4	63.50	x 0.33 =	20.96
FABRIC HEAT LOSS					Area m²	U-value W/m²K	
FLOOR		4.9	2.7		13.23	0.79	10.45
WALL		7.6		2.4	18.24	0.60	10.94
GLAZING (U = Glazing U - Wall U)		1.1		1.05	1.16	2.20	2.54
DOOR (U = Door U - Wall U)		1.75		2.10	3.66	2.20	8.09
ROOF							
ROOF GLAZING (U = Glazing U - Wall U)							
OTHER 1							
PARTY WALL (U = ½ of tabulated value)							

DESIGN ROOM TEMPERATURE	21		TOTAL HEAT LOSS/°C (W/K) *(sum of above)*	52.98
– OUTSIDE TEMPERATURE	-3			
= TEMPERATURE DIFFERENCE	24	→	x TEMPERATURE DIFFERENCE °C	24
			= DESIGN HEAT LOSS (W)	1272

EXPOSED LOCATION?	yes	If yes, add	10	% to design heat loss (see 8.5)	127
HIGH CEILING?	no	If yes, add	0	% to design heat loss (see 8.6)	0
INTERMITTENT HEATING		Add	10	% to design heat loss (see 8.8)	127
				Total room heat loss W *(enter on Worksheet 3)*	1526

41

10.0 RADIATORS AND OTHER HEAT EMITTERS

10.1 Emitter Types

Many different types of heat emitter are suitable for use in domestic heating systems, offering a range of options where space is restricted or low surface temperatures are required. However, steel panel radiators remain the most popular type in Britain and Ireland and are used in the sizing calculation examples that follow. Other types of heat emitter, such as underfloor heating, require special considerations for which the manufacturer's guidance should be followed.

10.2 Radiator Selection

The heat loss calculated for each room provides the basis for sizing the heat emitters, which must be capable of providing sufficient heat input to match the design heat loss. We use the example heat loss calculation in Section 9 to illustrate the method of sizing the radiator for the kitchen of the example house. The method described in this guide assumes that a two-pipe fully-pumped system will be used and should not be used for a single pipe system.

Similar calculations are made for all other rooms and the results are added to determine the total heat input required from the boiler and the sizing of the pipework, which will be dealt with in later sections.

10.3 Output Factors

Radiator output is principally by convection rather than by radiation and depends on a number of factors. It can vary considerably from the nominal output stated in the manufacturer's output tables according to the conditions under which the radiator is installed. The following factors determine the output.

- The difference between the mean temperature of the heating water and the room temperature, determines the rate at which heat from the water can be transferred to the room. This determines the value of factor **f1,** which is used to adjust the rated output of the emitter from the manufacturer's catalogue rating. The values of **f1** given below assume that the catalogue rating is based on a temperature difference of 60 degrees C, which is typically used by radiator manufacturers. Check that a different base temperature has not been used, in which case a correction will have to be made to take account of it.

- The connections from the main pipework to the radiator affect the output. The catalogue data for radiator output is based on the connections being made to top and bottom tappings at the same end of the radiator (TBSE). If any other configuration is used then factor **f2** must be applied. Bottom opposite end (BOE) connections, which are most frequently used in domestic installations, should have a connection factor of 0.96 applied.

- The positioning of a radiator (for example in a recess) affects its output and determines the value of factor **f3**. This factor also takes into account the reduced output as a result of encasing a radiator in a cabinet with top and bottom grilles. Low surface temperature kits have a similar effect and require the application of a factor, which should be obtained from the manufacturer.

- The surface finish of a radiator also affects its ability to emit heat, which is accounted for by factor **f4**. This normally needs to be applied when radiators are painted after installation; ordinary water or oil based paints will not affect the outputs but metallic paint can cause a reduction of 15%, which would result in **f4** being set to 0.85.

All factors are multiplied together to determine the Emission Factor **f**, which is applied to the manufacturer's catalogue data to give the actual output for the conditions under consideration.

10.4   Mean Water Temperature

The mean water temperature (MWT) of the water in the heating system is an important consideration to be determined by the designer. The greater the difference between the boiler flow and return temperatures, the less the flow required and the smaller the pipes. However, the return temperature and hence the mean temperature of the water will lower, requiring larger radiators.

Unless there are important reasons to the contrary, radiator systems should be designed using a 10°C temperature drop, as recommended in BS 5449. BS 5449 also requires that the boiler flow temperature should not exceed 82°C and should not be less than 66°C except for condensing boilers. Using the maximum flow temperature and the recommended temperature drop results in a return water of 72°C, a MWT of 77°C, and a 56°C difference from the recommended design room temperature.

Systems can be designed to operate at other temperatures depending on the type of equipment being used. Underfloor heating operates at much lower temperatures, for which guidance should be sought from manufacturers. Condensing boilers operate most efficiently with a low return temperature, which increases the amount of heat they can extract from flue gases.

10.5   Radiator Sizing

Radiator sizing can be undertaken using Worksheet Two - Emission Factors, and Worksheet Three - Radiator Selection..

The temperature difference identified in section 10.4 i.e. 56°C, may be used to determine the value of **f1**, by reference to Table 10.1. Factors **f2** to **f4**, for pipe connection, enclosure and paint finishes may be obtained from Tables 10.2 to 10.4 and the overall emission factor **f** by multiplying all of the individual factors together.   Factor **f** is then entered on Worksheet Three.

The radiators to heat each room can now be selected by using Worksheet Three - Radiator Selection. The calculated heat requirement for each room is taken from the appropriate Worksheet One. The factor **f** is taken from the appropriate Worksheet Two. Divide the calculated heat requirement by the emission factor **f** and compare the resulting heat output required with the manufacturers' output data. As **f** is typically somewhat less than 1, this results in the selection of radiators with a nominal heat output somewhat greater than the calculated heat loss. Different values of **f** may be needed for certain rooms if more than one type of heat emitter is to be used or if the temperature difference varies.

Radiators can now be chosen to suit the locations, taking account of the space available for mounting them and the shape and size of radiators available from particular manufacturers. An exact emission match will not always be available, so choose the radiator with the closest match, erring on the high side rather than the low side. Radiators should preferably be located under windows to reduce the effect of down draughts, and if possible relate to the width of the window. This may, however, be impractical if full-length curtains are to be used, which could result in much of the heat output going behind the curtains.

DOMESTIC HEATING DESIGN GUIDE WORKSHEET TWO – EMISSION FACTORS	
Boiler flow temperature (T_F)	82
System temperature drop (ΔT)	10
Mean water temperature (MWT = $T_F - (\Delta T/2)$)	77
Design room temperature (T_R)	21
Temperature difference (T_D = MWT $- T_R$)	56
f1 (*from table 10.1*)	0.918
f2 (*from table 10.2*)	0.96
f3 (*from table 10.3*)	0.95
f4 (*from table 10.4*)	1.0
f = f1 x f2 x f3 x f4 (*Enter on Worksheet Three*)	0.83

NOTE: Some Radiator Manufacturers base their Catalogue Outputs on a temperature difference other than 60°C. When this occurs adjust Factor f1 so that the specified temperature difference = 1.00.

$$f1 = \frac{\text{Actual temperature difference}^{1.24}}{\text{Catalogue temperature difference}}$$

Example. Where catalogue outputs are based on a 50⁰C difference

$$f1 = \frac{56}{50}^{1.24} = 1.51$$

TEMPERATURE DIFFERENCE FACTOR f_1

TD °C	f1	TD °C	f1
40	0.605	56	0.918
41	0.624	57	0.938
42	0.643	58	0.958
43	0.662	59	0.979
44	0.681	60	1.000
45	0.700	61	1.020
46	0.719	62	1.041
47	0.738	63	1.062
48	0.758	64	1.088
49	0.778	65	1.104
50	0.798	66	1.125
51	0.818	67	1.146
52	0.838	68	1.168
53	0.858	69	1.189
54	0.878	70	1.211
55	0.898	71	1.232

TABLE 10.1: VALUES FOR FACTOR f1

RADIATOR CONNECTION FACTOR	f_2
Top and bottom same end	1.00
Top and bottom opposite end	1.05
Bottom opposite end	0.96

TABLE 10.2: VALUES FOR FACTOR f2

ENCLOSURE FACTOR	f_3
Fixed on Plain Surface	1.00
Shelf over Radiator	0.95
Fixed in Open Recess	0.90
Encased in cabinet with front and top grille	0.80 to 0.70

TABLE 10.3: VALUES FOR FACTOR f3

PAINT FINISH FACTOR	f_4
Oil or Water based Paint	1.00
Metallic based Paint	0.85

TABLE 10.4: VALUES FOR FACTOR f4

10.6 Exposed Pipework Emissions

Where there are exposed pipes within a heated room, their heat output contributes to heating the room and may be deducted from the calculated room heat loss before the radiator size is arrived at. The output available from pipes can be calculated using Worksheet 4, which is on page 48.

After measuring the length and size of the pipes and recording this in the Worksheet, also enter the difference between the temperature of the water in the pipes and the air in the room under design conditions. The heat output from the exposed pipes may then be calculated using Table 10.5 and Table 10.6.

Table 10.5 gives the heat output per metre of pipe run for different pipe diameters against a series of temperature differences. The appropriate factor should be entered on the Worksheet. Table 10.6 gives values for the pipe configuration i.e. whether there is more than one pipe and whether the pipes are run vertically or horizontally. The appropriate value of **f5** is obtained from the Table and entered on the Worksheet. The final column of Worksheet 4 can be calculated by multiplying the length of pipe, the output per metre and the location factor. The adjusted pipework output for the room can now be entered on Worksheet 3.

If a room contains more than one type of pipe run, i.e. if there are both horizontal and vertical pipes or if there are pipes of different diameters, it will be necessary to enter these separately on Worksheet 4 and to add the totals together before transferring the amount to Worksheet 3.

PIPEWORK EMISSIONS IN W/M (painted copper pipe)							
	Temperature difference ^{o}C						
Pipe Size mm	50	55	56	59	61	65	70
8	19	21	22	24	25	27	31
10	23	27	28	30	31	34	39
15	35	40	41	44	46	51	58
22	40	56	57	61	64	71	80
28	64	72	74	79	82	91	110
35	76	87	89	96	101	110	122

PIPE LAYOUT	f_5
Single Pipe Horizontal	1.00
Double Pipe Horizontal	0.90
Vertical Up to 15mm dia.	0.75
Vertical 22mm and over	0.80

TABLE 10.5 PIPEWORK EMISSIONS

TABLE 10.6 PIPE LAYOUT FACTORS

10.7 Underfloor Heating

An underfloor heating system warms the floor structure, and thus the floor surface, which in turn warms the room or space. Warm air and floor duct systems are not considered to be underfloor heating systems in this context.

The main method of heat transfer from the heated floor surface is by radiation, which amounts to 50% to 60% of output. The balance is made up by convection and conduction. Because the majority of the heat is radiant it is very effective in creating comfort at slightly lower temperatures than would be expected from a radiator or convector system. A correctly designed and installed system causes virtually no air convection currents or temperature stratification such as is associated with other types of space heating system.

There is also a benefit in fuel economy, as high temperatures at high level in a room, which result from strong convection currents, are absent. Having the feet very slightly warmer than the head is considered to give optimum comfort conditions. If, however, an underfloor system is used only for short periods and at infrequent intervals, other systems may return lower running costs, particularly if a screed or solid floor system is used.

The basic principle of operation of a 'wet' underfloor heating system is that heated water is circulated through pipes, which are usually of plastic or plastic metal composite, and are buried into the floor structure. The floor structure must either be conductive itself or conductive elements need to be embedded into the floor to transfer the heat from the pipes to the floor surface.

Because the floor surface area is large, compared to the size of a steel panel radiator, the floor surface temperature required is usually quite low and very close to the actual room temperature. It should, however, be at or below 29° C in all occupied areas so as to achieve an acceptable degree of foot comfort. Lower temperature limits, such as 27°C for timber floors, are sometimes required for delicate structures or surface finishes.

It is essential that floor coverings do not provide too great a degree of insulation or the heat in the underfloor system may not be able to raise the room temperature to its design level. Care is required, particularly with underlay used with fitted carpets and with laminate floor systems.

Any boiler or heat generator can be used as many systems are fed through mixing headers. For direct connection condensing boilers and heat pumps can benefit in efficiency from the lower flow and return water temperatures normally used in underfloor systems.

The overall design of underfloor heating systems is undertaken in accordance with Standard BS EN 1264 Parts 1,2,3 and 4.

The Underfloor Heating Design and Installation Guide, also published by the CIBSE Domestic Building Services Panel, gives full information on the subject.

DOMESTIC HEATING DESIGN GUIDE
WORKSHEET THREE – RADIATOR SELECTION

Room	Design temp °C	Heat losses (from Work-sheet One) W	Pipework emissions (from Work-sheet Four) W	Nett heat output required from radiator (heat losses minus pipework emissions) W	Emission factor f (from Worksheet Two)	Radiator listed output required (nett heat output divided by emission factor) W	Radiator selection (from catalogue)	Catalogue listed output W	Actual calculated output (catalogue output multiplied by emission factor) W
LOUNGE	21	1526		1526	0.83	1839	S600 x 1500	2000	1660
KIT / DINING	21	1593		1593	0.83	1919	D600 X 950	2050	1702
HALL / LANDING	21	1158	154	1004	0.83	1210	D600 X 550	1215	1008
BATHROOM	22	616		616	0.81	760	S600 X 650	800	648
BEDROOM 1	21	975		975	0.83	1174	S500 X 1100	1190	987
BEDROOM 2	21	630		630	0.83	759	S500 X 750	800	664
Totals W		6498		6344					6669

DOMESTIC HEATING DESIGN GUIDE
WORKSHEET FOUR – EXPOSED PIPEWORK EMISSIONS

| Room | Temp. diff. (water to air) °C | Pipe Emission | | | | Total pipe emission (PE) W |
		Size mm	Length (L) m	Output (from Table 10.5) W/m	Location factor f$_5$ (from Table 10.6)	
Hall	56	15	5.0	41	0.75	154

11.0   BOILERS

11.1   Boiler Output

The boiler must have sufficient output to meet its maximum load, which includes the radiators, the domestic hot water cylinder and the heat losses from the distribution pipework. It should also have sufficient extra capacity to warm the house up in a reasonable time when the system is switched on from cold. It should not be oversized, however, as that will increase its capital cost. Oversizing can also adversely affect efficiency and hence running cost, although most modern boilers are capable of operating efficiently under part load conditions.

11.2   Boiler Sizing Method

Worksheet Five - Boiler Sizing enables a boiler with the required output for both space and water heating to be selected. The required boiler output for space heating may be derived from the addition of all of the total heat loads shown in column 3 of Worksheet Three. It is not necessary to make a further allowance for intermittent heating as that has already been included in the calculations for the individual rooms.

For combination boilers, it is likely that the power required for water heating will exceed that for space heating, which may be checked by comparing the total heat load with the boiler's rated output. For regular boilers, an allowance should be made for domestic hot water where that is produced from the central heating system. The power required to heat the entire contents of the hot water cylinder rapidly is high (as shown in column 3 of Table 12.1) but that will rarely be required at the same time as the maximum space heating load. However, an allowance for water heating is recommended as shown in column 4 of the table for different sizes of dwelling.

Where distribution pipework is located entirely within the heated space of the dwelling, losses from pipework may be ignored. When losses are incurred outside the heated space, such as when the boiler is located in a garage or an outdoor enclosure, add 10% to the total calculated for space heating.

DOMESTIC HEATING DESIGN GUIDE
WORKSHEET FIVE – BOILER SIZING

Boiler size calculation	Watts
Total heat loss from rooms	
Distribution losses *(add 10% if required)*	
Hot water allowance *(from Table 12.1)*	
Total heat load to be met by boiler	

12.0   DOMESTIC HOT WATER SUPPLY

12.1   Hot Water Sources

Domestic hot water can be supplied either from a pre-heated stored supply or heated at the time of use. For the central heating system designer, the key choice lies between a regular boiler, with a separate hot water storage cylinder, and a combination boiler, which heats water when it is required. There are also other systems, which provide various combinations of storage and instantaneous heat generation. For example, some combination boilers incorporate storage for a limited amount of hot water. Other types include direct fired water storage heaters, thermal stores units and combined primary storage units.

12.2   Choice of System

A number of factors need to be considered when choosing which type of hot water system to install and it is essential the client understands the characteristics of the various options. The main requirements to be considered are:

- the volume of hot water required; and
- the flow-rate and dynamic pressure[3] at which it needs to be delivered.

Both of these requirements are related to the number of people expected to live in the house and the number of baths/showers that may be in use simultaneously. The choice of system must also take account of the space available in the house for hot water storage and whether or not it is important to have a dry loft, containing no cisterns or water pipes. For all systems that supply hot water directly at mains pressure, including combination boilers and thermal stores, it is particularly important to ensure that the incoming water supply to the dwelling has adequate dynamic pressure and flow at times of maximum demand. Note that the performance of mains pressure water heaters is specified in terms of temperature rise above the temperature of the incoming water supply.

In the Republic of Ireland, Part G of the Building Regulations requires that only the kitchen sink may be connected directly to the incoming cold water supply, which effectively prohibits the use of combination boilers, thermal stores and unvented hot water storage vessels.

Size of Dwelling	Minimum capacity of cylinder (litres)	Power req. for 1-hour heat-up 10-60° (kW)	Extra boiler allowance for heat-up (kW) (enter on Worksheet Five)
2 Bed,1 Bath	125	7.2	2.0
3 Bed,1 Bath	145	8.4	2.5
4 Bed ,1 Bath	145	8.4	2.5
4 Bed, 1 Bath, 1 shower	175	10.0	2.5
4 Bed, 2 Bath	225	13.0	3.0

TABLE 12.1 RECOMMENDED STORAGE VOLUMES

---

[3] Dynamic pressure is defined as the pressure sustained at a given flow rate.

12.3 Hot Water Storage Cylinders

Where an indirect cylinder is used to store domestic hot water, the heat required from the boiler for water heating must be considered when determining the boiler capacity required. Table 12.1 shows recommended storage volumes for double feed indirect cylinders with pumped primary connections.

The heat up time of a cylinder full of water depends on the surface area of the heating coil, the available boiler capacity, the size and configuration of the primary pipework and the control arrangement. Most standard indirect cylinders served with pumped primary water are capable of heating the contents in 30 minutes or less, which is adequate for a dwelling with normal occupancy. High performance cylinders, with a fast recovery heat exchanger, can be used to achieve better performance without increasing cylinder size. Note, however, that some fast recovery cylinders may require higher pressure to achieve the full design flow rate through the coil.

The height of the cold water storage cistern above the cylinder governs the static pressure, from which pipe sizes and the grade of construction for the cylinder may be determined. Cylinder grades are shown in Table 12.2.

Grade Number	Test Pressure bar	Maximum Working Pressure (Static Head) m
1	3.65	25
2	2.20	15
3	1.45	10
4	1.00	5

TABLE 12.2: HOT WATER CYLINDER GRADES

12.4 Combination Boilers

Combination boilers can save space in two ways: they need no hot water storage cylinder or cistern as they are fed directly from the cold water supply; and they are usually intended for use in a sealed primary system, with no feed/expansion cistern. Another advantage of combination boilers is that they provide the option of a dry loft, as they need no cisterns to be placed there to provide the necessary pressures. The same attribute can be especially helpful in a flat, where there may be no opportunity to obtain adequate pressure from a cold water cistern.

The limitations of combination boilers for hot water supply should also be understood by both the installer and the client. In particular, the client should be aware of:

- the time taken for the hot water to reach an acceptable temperature;

- the maximum flow rate at which hot water can be drawn off, especially for a sustained period, for example when filling a bath;

- susceptibility to scaling by hard water;

- the inability to fit an immersion heater for back-up hot water supply; and

- the limitations of flow rate when serving more than one point simultaneously.

Combination boilers with internal hot water stores can go a long way towards overcoming these difficulties, particularly if they have a storage volume large enough for a bath. However, a large storage volume must inevitably increase the size of the boiler itself and may make it too large to fit in the space available. For a combination boiler, the power required for acceptable hot water service is typically well in excess of that required for space heating. Because there is no hot water cylinder, pipework and controls are considerably simplified. Otherwise the design procedures and layouts for space heating are as described in chapter 13.

In large houses, it may be appropriate to use a combination boiler to provide part of the hot water requirement (for example to the kitchen and downstairs cloakroom) and to install a hot water storage cylinder to provide the rest (for example to upstairs bathrooms). Combination boiler systems comprise over half of all domestic installations.

12.5 Thermal Stores and Combined Primary Storage Units

Thermal stores are vessels containing a volume of primary water which can be heated to a flow temperature of 82°C either by a separate boiler or by direct firing. By so doing they aim to produce a rapid response when the system is turned on. Some thermal stores are for hot water only while others, known as integrated thermal stores, are also coupled to the space heating. Combined primary storage units (CPSUs) embody the functions of both a boiler and a thermal store, containing both elements within the same casing. Both thermal stores and CPSUs produce domestic hot water through heat exchangers at mains pressure, so, like combination boilers, they can be used in situations where it is difficult to achieve satisfactory pressure from a storage cistern. However, they do not match the compactness of combination boilers, as they are generally fairly bulky.

A thermal store can be used in a system either with two or more circulators controlled by the cylinder and room thermostats, or with a single circulator and diverter valve, as shown in Figure 12.1. When using the two circulator system the boiler should be set at maximum temperature (82°C) at all times and the hot water cylinder thermostat set approx. 4°C lower at 78°C. It should be noted that there will be a reduced flow temperature from the thermal storage cylinder which will result in a lower mean water temperature (approx. 73°C) and may require increases in the sizes of the radiators.

As with unvented cylinders, site requirements and installation instructions for thermal storage cylinders vary from one manufacturer to another and cannot be specifically defined in this text. The manufacturer's instructions should be carefully followed to ensure correct installation. There is no requirement to notify the Local Authority when installing a thermal storage unit in the United Kingdom.

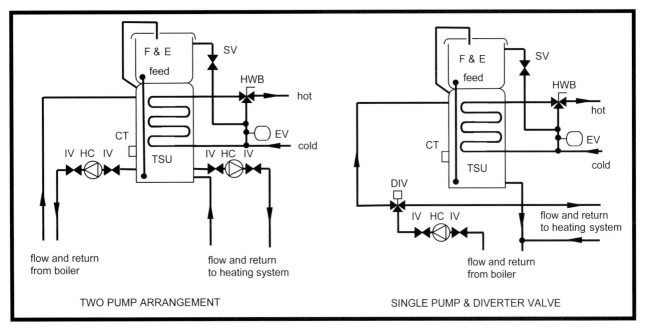

TWO PUMP ARRANGEMENT   SINGLE PUMP & DIVERTER VALVE

Fig 12.1 CIRCULATOR ARRANGEMENTS FOR THERMAL STORES

12.6   Secondary Circulation

On larger installations, long pipe runs to draw-off points can cause a significant amount of water to have to be drawn off before an acceptable temperature is reached. Secondary pumped circulation, using a bronze pump, can be used to overcome that problem; a typical circuit is shown in shown in Figure 12.2. It should be noted, however, that secondary circulation adds to the amount of heat required by the cylinder and, especially when fitted with towel rails, increases the cylinder heat up time. All pipework on the secondary circulation should be insulated to prevent heat loss and maintain a high water temperature at the tap outlets.

It is not possible to install secondary circulation with a thermal storage cylinder. Also, it is not recommended when Economy 7 electricity is only heat source, since a heat top-up will be required during the day due to the heat which will be lost from the circulation pipes, even when insulated.

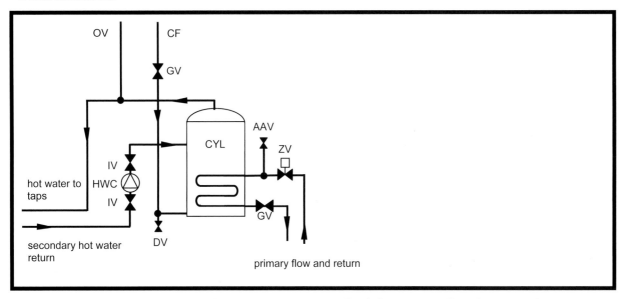

FIG 12.2 INDIRECT CYLINDER WITH SECONDARY CIRCULATION

12.7 Trace Heating

Trace heating, using electric elements, can be used as an alternative to secondary circulation, with the advantage that no circulation pump or return pipework is needed. Good insulation of secondary pipework is especially important with trace heating, given the high unit cost of the electricity used to produce the heat.

12.8 Unvented Hot Water Cylinders

Unvented domestic hot water systems use water direct from the incoming supply and do not require a cold water storage cistern. They have been in common use in countries throughout the world for many years and are now gaining popularity in the UK, although they are not permitted in the Republic of Ireland. Unvented cylinders generally provide very good flow characteristics and the pressure balance with cold water supply makes them particularly attractive for showers.

Fig. 12.3 shows the components required for a typical system, including the necessary safety components. Safety is a prime consideration when specifying an unvented hot water system and there are a number of mandatory requirements:

- When an unvented hot water cylinder is supplied with primary water from a sealed heating system the boiler output rating must not exceed 45kW.

- **Building regulations in the United Kingdom require that the authority responsible for building control is notified before an unvented cylinder of over 15 litres capacity is installed.**

- All installations must be carried out by a "competent person" and all cylinders must be on the Approved List of the British Board of Agrément.

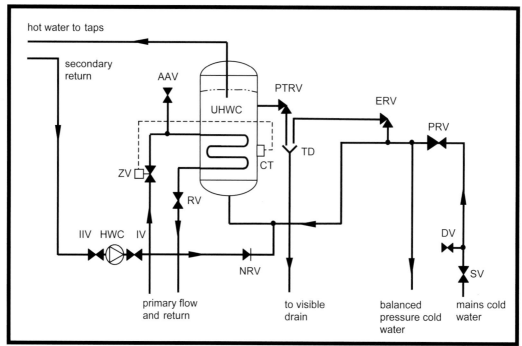

FIG 12.3   UNVENTED HOT WATER CYLINDER

12.9   Hard Water

In hard water areas where the temporary hardness of the water exceeds 200 mg/l, it is recommended consideration be given to treating the incoming mains water supply with a suitable base-exchange water softener so that all equipment is protected and the client has the advantage of using softened water. If a water softener is to be used, it is necessary to make sure that there is sufficient mains water pressure to overcome the typical pressure drop of the softener which can be up to one bar. Alternatively an in-line scale reducer or ion-exchange unit can be fitted on the cold water supply to the water heater/cylinder, or on the cold supply main to the property. Protection against hard water is particularly important for combination boilers and thermal stores, in which water is heated at the time of use and high temperatures are involved.

12.10 Dead Legs

The length of hot water draw off pipework to taps and other outlets should be kept to a minimum to reduce the amount of cold water drawn off before the hot water appears. The maximum recommended dead-leg lengths are shown in Table 12.3. Where there is more than one size of pipe on a dead-leg, the equivalent length and size should be estimated.

When the dead-leg length exceeds the recommended maximum, secondary circulation or trace heating should be installed, controlled by a time-switch and incorporating a motorised valve to stop gravity circulation.

Pipe size (mm)	Maximum length (m)
10,12	20
15,22	12
28	8
35 and above	3

TABLE 12.3: MAXIMUM RECOMMENDED PIPE RUNS FOR HOT WATER DRAW-OFF

13.0 SYSTEM LAYOUTS

13.1 Typical System Layout

Fig 13.1 shows a typical fully pumped[4] system. It uses a three-way motorised valve to provide water to the heating system or domestic hot water cylinder as and when required. Similar operation can be obtained by using two 2 port valves. Refer to section 18 of this Guide for a description of the application of controls to different circuit layouts.

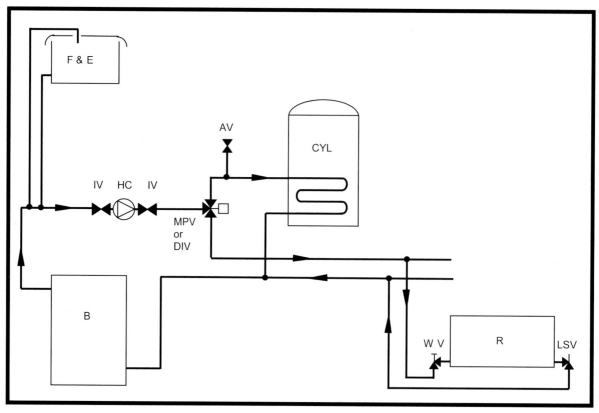

FIG 13.1 HEATING AND DOMESTIC HOT WATER USING A MID-POSITION OR DIVERTER VALVE

13.2 One-pipe Circuits

The recommendations in this publication do not apply to one-pipe systems. One-pipe circuits require careful design to take account of reducing water temperature along the circuit, which reduces radiator outputs and hence affects their sizing.

---

[4] The term 'fully pumped' is generally used to describe a system that relies entirely on a mechanical circulator for its circulation, as opposed to systems that rely wholly or partly or thermo-siphoning, which are known as 'gravity' or 'semi-gravity' systems.

13.3 Reverse Return System

A **reverse return** layout is shown in Fig.13.2. This is a variation of the conventional two-pipe circuit, which has the advantage of equalising the pressure loss to all parts of the system. This layout is particularly useful when installing two boilers, as it helps to ensure both receive equal amounts of the water being circulated. It can be seen from the figure that the total length of the flow and return pipework from the branch tees is equal to both boilers.

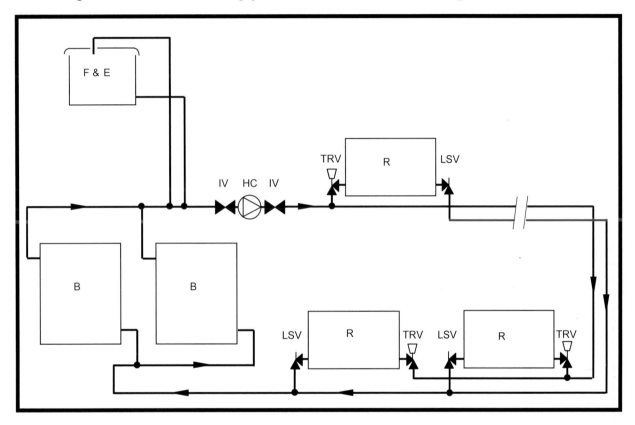

FIG. 13.2   REVERSE RETURN HEATING CIRCUIT

13.4 Avoiding Reversed Circulation

The reverse return layout shown in Figure 13.2 should not be confused with the phenomenon of reversed circulation, which causes radiators to heat when only the water heating circuit should be operating. It can be diagnosed by the temperature reversal of flow and return to some of the radiators and is the result of the return path for those radiators being shared with the hot water primary circuit, as shown in Figure 13.3. The problem is easily avoided by ensuring that all heating circuits are taken from a common flow and all heating returns are joined to a common return before being connected to the return from the hot water cylinder.

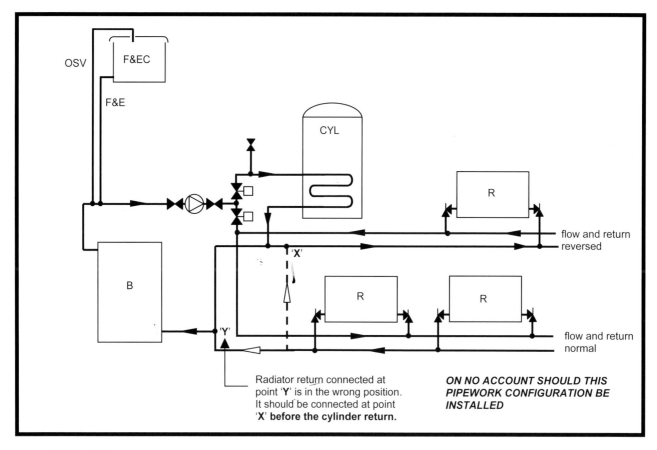

FIG. 13.3

13.5 Pipework Sizing

Heating system pipework must be sized so that each part of the circuit has sufficient circulation to deliver its rated heat output. The flow required for each heat emitter is directly related to its output and may be calculated using the design temperature difference. The pressure required to achieve circulation depends upon the resistance to flow in the circuit, which is affected by pipe length and diameter, the number and type of fittings and the resistance of components including the boiler and heat exchangers. The designer's task is to ensure that the circuit resistance is low enough for the circulator (pump) to achieve the required flow to all points in the circuit, without undue noise or a tendency to collect air in parts of the system. In particular, the circulator has to be capable of overcoming the resistance of the circuit with the highest resistance – the "index circuit" – at the same time as providing the necessary flow required by the whole system.

13.6 The Design Method

The following step-by-step method is recommended to achieve optimum pipe sizing. It uses the design temperature difference and the heat flow required to calculate the flow of primary water required for each part of the circuit. Pipe sizes are then chosen to avoid excessive flow velocities and pressure drops calculated for their path around the circuit. The steps are as follows:

1. Sketch the circuit, showing all system components and pipework as shown in Figure 13.4 on page 64. Mark up the pipe sections using the identifying letters at the junctions. These will need to be also entered in column one of Worksheet 7, see page 61. At the same time measure the pipe lengths from the drawings and enter these in column four of Worksheet 7.

2. On Worksheet 6, page 60, list all the heat emitters together with their respective heat outputs. The flow rates necessary to achieve the rated outputs are obtained using the calculation shown in Section 13.9 on page 63. Flow rates can then be transferred to column two of Worksheet 7.

3. Using Table 13.2 on page 63 make an initial estimate of the pipe size for each part of the circuit and enter it on Worksheet 6. This information can then be transferred to column three of Worksheet 7. More information is given in Section 13.7 below.

4. Using Worksheet 7 calculate the pressure loss for each part of the circuit from the required flow rate and the selected pipe size, using Table 13.1 on page 62. This will give the pressure loss in metres head per metre run of pipe (m/m), which is entered in column five. This figure is multiplied by the pipe length in metres from column four. This will give the total pressure loss in metres (m) for that part of the circuit, which is then entered in column six. More information is given in Sections 13.8, below and 13.10 on page 64.

5. On Worksheet 7 identify the 'index circuit', which is the path around the system that requires the greatest pressure to achieve the necessary flow. More information is given in Section 13.11 on page 64.

6. Make allowances for the pressure loss through pipe fittings, any by-pass and the boiler, before completing Worksheet 7.

7. Compare the pressure required by the index circuit, and the total flow required by the system with the circulator characteristics supplied by the manufacturer. See Figure 14.1 on page 66.

8. Make adjustments to the pipe sizes if it is necessary to adjust the pressure loss to fit pump capacity, and repeat steps 4 to 6.

13.7 Initial Size Estimate

Use Table 13.1 to make an initial estimate of pipe size required for each part of the circuit, ensuring that the flow rate is no greater than 1.5 metres/second, as specified in BS 5449. This will assist in avoiding the noises that can be created by water flowing at higher velocities. Alternatively, an initial estimate of the pipe size can be taken from the Table 13.2 for 'Quick Sizing'.

13.8 Frictional Resistance

For systems up to 45kW output, calculate pressure drops for pipework, allowing between 33% and 50% extra for the resistance of standard radiators and fittings. Modern boilers tend to have a fairly high flow resistance, as do certain types of heat emitter, such as fan convectors, so their pressure drops need to be calculated in addition to pipework and fittings. The necessary pressure loss characteristics should be taken from manufacturer's data.

DOMESTIC HEATING DESIGN GUIDE

WORKSHEET SIX – FLOW RATE AND PIPE SIZE

Room	Radiator output required (from work-sheet three) W	Emiss-ions from exposed pipe W	Combined output from radiators and exposed pipe W	10% heat loss from mains W	Total heat loss W	Flow rate kg/s	Initially selected pipe diameter mm
Lounge	1660	-	1660	166	1826	0.044	10
Kit/Dining	1702	-	1702	170	1872	0.045	10
Hall/ Landing	1008	154	1162	116	1278	0.031	8
Bathroom	648	-	648	65	713	0.017	8
Bedroom 1	987	-	987	99	1086	0.026	8
Bedroom 2	664	-	664	66	730	0.017	8
H W Cylinder					2000	0.048	22

Revisions

DOMESTIC HEATING DESIGN GUIDE
WORKSHEET SEVEN – PRESSURE LOSS

Pipe section	Flow rate kg/s	Selected pipe diameter mm	Length of flow and return pipes in metres m	Pressure loss in metres per metre run m/m	Total pressure loss metres head m	Comments
a-g	0.044	10	8.0	0.094	0.752	
g-h	0.070	15	3.5	0.024	0.084	
h-i	0.101	15	8.0	0.046	0.368	
i-k	0.118	15	2.0	0.061	0.122	
Total a-k					1.326	Use for index circuit
f-j	0.045	10	7.0	0.098	0.686	
j-k	0.062	15	10.0	0.020	0.200	
Total f-k					0.886	Less than a-k ∴ use a-k
Index Circuit						
a-k	0.118				1.326	from above
k-l	0.180	22	3.0	0.020	0.060	Keep same size as mid-position valve (22)
l-m	0.228	22	9.0	0.030	0.270	
			Index circuit Sub. total		1.656	
Flow rate sub. total	0.228		Allowance for fittings 50% of sub. total		0.828	
Add bypass (if fitted)	0.10		Other allowances		0.275	Boiler
Total flow rate	0.328	kg/s	**Total pressure loss**		2.759	**Metres head**

Pressure loss (m/m)	8 mm kg/s	10 mm kg/s	15 mm kg/s	22 mm kg/s	28 mm kg/s	35 mm kg/s	Velocity m/s
0.008		0.0108	.0380	0.109	0.227	0.400	0.50
0.009		0.0114	0.040	0.117	0.235	0.424	
0.010	0.0064	0.0122	0.042	0.124	0.250	0448	
0.011	0 0067	0 0129	0.044	0.131	0.263	0.475	
0.012	0.0071	0.0135	0.047	0.137	0.277	0.499	
0.013	0.0074	0.0141	0.049	0.144	0.289	0.523	
0.014	0.0077	0.0147	0.052	0.150	0.302	0.543	
0.015	0.0081	0.0154	0.054	0.156	0.314	0.564	
0.016	0.0084	0.0159	0.056	0.161	0.325	0.594	
0.017	0.0086	0.0165	0.058	0.167	0.336	0.604	0.75
0.018	0.0089	0.0171	0.060	0.172	0.348	0.623	
0.019	0.0092	0.0176	0.061	0.178	0.359	0.645	
0.020	0.0095	0.0182	0.063	0.183	0.369	0.669	
0.021	0.0098	0.0185	0.065	0.188	0.380	0.686	
0.022	0.0101	0.0192	0.067	0.193	0.390	0.704	
0.024	0.0106	0.0203	0.070	0.203	0.408	0.735	
0.026	0.0111	0.0212	0.073	0.212	0.428	0.773	
0.028	0.0116	0.0221	0.076	0.221	0.446	0.805	1.00
0.030	0.0120	0.0230	0.080	0.230	0.464	0.838	
0.032	0.0125	0.0238	0.082	0.238	0.482	0.869	
0.034	0.0129	0.0245	0.085	0.247	0.500	0.898	
0.036	0.0133	0.0253	0.088	0.255	0.518	0.925	
0.038	0.0138	0.0261	0.091	0.263	0.533	0.952	
0.040	0.0142	0.0268	0.094	0.270	0.548	0.982	
0.042	0.0146	0.0276	0.096	0.278	0.564	1.010	1.25
0.044	0.0150	0.0283	0.099	0.286	0.578	1.035	
0.046	0.0154	0.0290	0.101	0.293	0.592	1.048	
0.048	0.0158	0.0298	0.104	0.300	0.608	1.075	
0.050	0.0162	0.0305	0.106	0.307	0.622	1.100	
0.052	0.0167	0.0312	0.018	0.314	0.637	1.123	
0.054	0.0170	0.0320	0.111	0.321	0.651	1.150	
0.056	0.0173	0.0326	0.113	0.328	0.665	1.178	
0.058	0.0177	0.0332	0.115	0.334	0678	1.194	1.50
0.060	0.0180	0.0339	0.117	0.340	0.691	1.215	
0.062	0.0184	0.0345	0.120	0.347	0.705	1.235	
0.064	0.0187	0.0351	0.122	0.353	0.718	1.253	
0.066	0.0190	0.0358	0.124	0.359	0.724	1.272	
0.068	0.0193	0.0364	0.126	0.364	0.736		
0.070	0.0196	0.0370	0.128	0.370	0.750		
0.072	0.0200	0.0377	0.130	0.375	0.762		
0.074	0.0203	0.0382	0.132	0.381	0.774		
0.076	0.0206	0.0388	0.134	0.386	0.785		
0.078	0.0208	0.0394	0.136	0.391	0.797		
0.080	0.0211	0.0400	0.138	0.397	0.808		
0.082	0.0215	0.0406	0.140	0.402	0.819		
0.084	0.0217	0.0411	0.142	0.407	0.830		
0.086	0.0220	0.0417	0.144	0.412	0.841		
0.088	0.0223	0.0423	0.146	0.417	0.851		
0.090	0.0226	0.0429	0.148	0.422	0.862		
0.092	0.0229	0.0433	0. 149	0.426	0.872		
0.094	0.0231	0.0439	0.151	0.431			
0.096	0.0234	0.0445	0.153	0.435			
0.098	0.0237	0.0450	0.155	0.440			
0.100	0.0240	0.0455	0.156	0.445			
0.102	0.0243	0.0460	0.158	0.449			
0.104	0.0245	0.0465	0.160	0.453			
0.106	0.0247	0.0469	0.162	0.458			
0.108	0.0250	0.0474	0.164	0.462			
0.110	0.0253	0.0479	0.165	0.466			
0.112	0.0256	0.0484	0.167	0.471			
0.114	0.0258	0.0488	0.169	0.475			
0.116	0.0261	0.0493	0.170	0.479			
0.118	0.0264	0.0498	0.172				
0.120	0.0266	0.0502	0.174				
0.130	0.0279	0.0523	0.181				
0.140	0.0291	0.0548	0.189				
0.150	0.0302	0.0568	0.197				
0.160	0.0314	0.0588	0.204				
0. 170	0.0326	0.0608	0.211				
0.180	0.0336	0.0628					
0.190	0.0347	0.0648					
0.200	0.0357	0.0668					

TABLE 13.1: FLOW OF WATER IN COPPER TUBES

Copper Pipe Diameter (mm)	Approx. Loading W
8	1500
10	2500
15	6000
22	13000
28	22000
35	34000

TABLE 13.2: QUICK PIPEWORK SIZING

13.9 Pipework Sizing Example

The pipework layout on the terraced house example shown on Page 40 is shown in simplified form in the line schematic diagram in Figure 13.4, with room names and the individual sections of pipe defined using the letters 'a' to 'm'. This is done by taking the radiator and exposed pipework outputs and adding an allowance of 10% for the losses from the distribution pipework. The result is then used in the following equation to establish the flow rate of water through the pipe, expressed in kilograms per second (kg/s).

Flow rate = H / (TD x SH) kg/sec,   where

H is the heat output of the radiator and exposed pipework in Watts,
TD is the temperature difference between flow and return in °C and
SH is the specific heat of water in J/kg.

For example, the flow rate to the radiator in Bedroom 1 is given by:

Flow rate = 1086/ (10 x 4187) kg/sec.
            = 0.026 kg/sec

(The specific heat of water is 4187 joules/kg)

The flow rates to the radiators are then used to select initial pipe sizes, using Table 13.1 and Worksheet 6. The results are also shown on the schematic layout diagram in Figure 13.4.

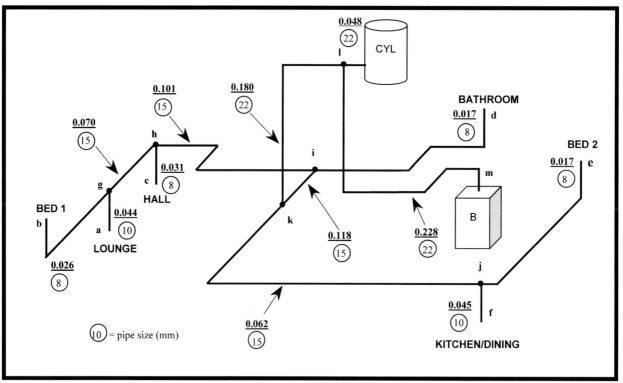

Note: Underlined figures are flow rate in kg/sec

FIG 13.4 SCHEMATIC LAYOUT

13.10 Pressure Loss Calculations

The pressure loss in the pipework may now be calculated for every section of the circuit, starting at the end radiators and working back towards the boiler, using Worksheet Seven. The length of the flow and return pipework for each individual circuit may be measured from the plan. The pipe sizes and flow rates are taken from Worksheet Six, and the pressure loss per metre taken from Table 13.1.

Table 13.1 shows the pressure loss expressed in metres of water per metre run of pipe (m/m) for copper tube to BS EN 1254. Data for pipes made of other materials such as plastic, stainless steel or mild steel, should be obtained from their suppliers. Other sources may express pressure loss in different units such as pascals/metre – always use compatible units in any calculation. *(1 metre of water = 9807 Pa).*

Where polybutylene and polyethylene pipe is to be used, the internal diameter of the pipe will be less than that for copper tube to BS EN 1254 and therefore frictional resistance (pressure losses) will be higher for given flow rates. Refer to manufacturers' literature.

13.11 Index Circuit Selection

It is not obvious at this stage which is the index circuit: the pipework to the radiator in the lounge, or that to the kitchen/dining room. To decide which it should be, compare the pressure drop in each circuit up to the point where they join together (a - k and f - k), using the information in Worksheet Seven. The greater pressure drop occurs in the lounge circuit, which identifies it as the index circuit, along with the common section (l – m).

The total flow rate and pressure loss calculated may now be compared with circulator characteristics so that the correct size of circulator can be selected. (see Section 14)

There may be occasions when it will be necessary to make changes at this stage. For example, the pressure loss in a particular section of pipe may turn out to be unduly high, or the size of the boiler connecting pipework does not conform to the manufacturer's requirements. In such cases, the size must be altered and the total resistance recalculated. Otherwise, pipe sizing is now complete.

13.12 Cylinder Connections

Hot water cylinders should have primary pipework of at least 22mm diameter, which will ensure low pressure loss and rapid cylinder temperature recovery..

13.13 Quick Pipework Sizing

The information in Table 13.2 should only be used for pipework on pumped systems and the loadings should include a suitable margin, say 10%, for pipework heat losses. It should only be used as a guide to the sizing of pipework for estimating purposes and should not be used to determine the installed pipework specification.

The sizes do not take into account the total circulator pressure available for the system or the temperature drop required by any specific item of equipment, or for any specific pipework connection sizes required by items such as the boiler, etc.

14.0 CIRCULATOR SELECTION

14.1 Circulator Sizing

The pressure loss calculations undertaken to size the pipework provide the necessary basis for specifying the circulator needed to provide the flow of water around the system. Figure 14.1 shows a typical circulator performance chart, giving the relationship between circulator flow rate and the pressure against which the circulator is operating. The flow-rate and pressure required by the system may be taken from Worksheet 7. The design pressure and flow for the system should be super-imposed on the circulator performance chart for comparison with the circulator characteristics. The circulator normally has a number of settings; choose the lowest setting able to generate sufficient flow at the design pressure.

If the circulator is too small or on too low a setting, then the flow rate will be less than required. That will cause the system to operate at below design return temperature and it will then fail to deliver the required heat output. If the circulator is set too high, then flow rate and return temperature will both be above design values, which may cause excessive noise and will unnecessarily increase the electricity consumed by the circulator itself.

Circulators are also available with automatic self-adjustment. These incorporate an electronic control circuit that can continuously adjust pumping power to maintain pressure appropriate to the demands of the moment, for example when thermostatic radiator valves restrict the flow to individual radiators. The benefits include easier initial setting-up, reduced noise and reduced electricity consumption in use. (See also 14.8)

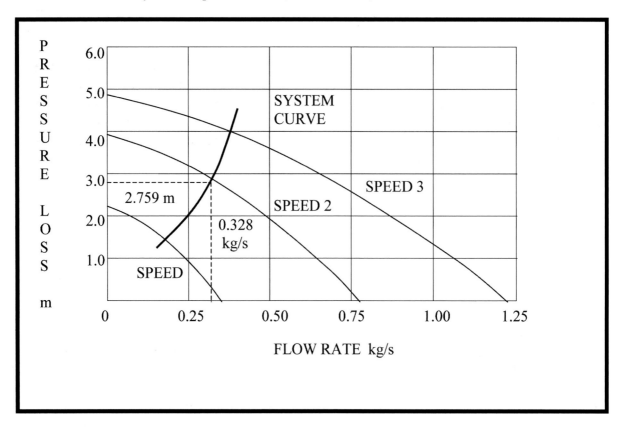

FIG 14.1   CIRCULATOR PERFORMANCE CURVE

66

14.2 Worked Example

In the example, the circulator is required to produce a system total flow of 0.328 kg/s, or 0.328 litres/s (since 1 litre of water weighs 1 kg), against a resistance in its index circuit of 2.759 m, or 27.06 kPa (since 1m head equals 9.807 kPa). When compared with the circulator performance curve, it may be observed that the point defined by the calculated system flow and index pressure falls somewhat below the line corresponding to the No.2 speed setting. (See Figure 14.1)

By following the system curve, it can be seen that the No 2 speed setting will provide rather more than the required flow and should be selected. At the No 1 speed setting the circulator would deliver insufficient circulation, and at the No 3 setting would produce a significantly larger flow than needed. In general, choose the lowest setting able to provide the required flow or the minimum flow specified in the boiler manufacturer's instructions, whichever is the larger.

14.3 Circulator Position

The circulator should be installed to maintain a positive pressure at all points around the system and, when fitted to an open vented system, be subject to at least the minimum static pressure specified by the manufacturer. This is defined in BS 5449 as being one third of the maximum pressure developed by the circulator under no water flow conditions. For most domestic circulators this is between 1.7 and 2.0 metres of water.

The circulator should not be located at the lowest part of a system, where it is possible for sediment to collect, nor at the highest point, where air can be a problem.

Circulator installation should observe manufacturer's instructions about the orientation of the installation. This normally requires that the circulator should be located with it's motor shaft in a horizontal position so that there is no undue load on the bearings, and should either be fixed into a vertical pipe so that the water is flowing upward, or in a horizontal position. It is often difficult to remove trapped air from the impeller casing and for this reason a circulator should not be installed facing vertically downwards.

14.4 System Fault Diagnosis

System design faults or abuse can often be diagnosed from the sediment found in the circulator. They are usually either black encrustation (ferric oxide) or a red sediment (ferrous oxide).

The black ferric oxide is often as a result of the system not having been flushed out correctly on completion of the installation, leaving extraneous matter in the water and causing the residue to form hydrogen which has to be vented out of the system.

The red ferrous oxide is caused by air entering the system, possibly being entrained on the suction side of the circulator or from the feed and expansion cistern on an open vented system. This is commonly the result of incorrect positioning of the feed and venting pipework in relation to the circulator, resulting in failure to maintain a positive pressure at all points in the system. In such circumstances, the circulator is likely to fail, often followed by leaking radiators and heat exchangers.

14.5 Boiler Noise

Boilers with high efficiency usually have a low water content and require a minimum flow rate to be maintained through the heat exchanger to ensure the heat can be removed quickly enough. Small systems, which do not require a high circulator duty, can occasionally cause noise problems if the boiler requirement for a minimum flow rate is overlooked. In such cases, an automatic bypass valve should be fitted so that the minimum water quantity can flow through the boiler without relying on circulation through the radiators. In these circumstances the circulator must be capable of satisfying the duty of both the system and the bypass.

A boiler operating with inadequate flow through it is said to 'kettle', a description derived from the characteristic noise it makes. If allowed to operate in this manner too long before remedial action is taken, it will probably have a deposit of calcium in the heat transfer coil which will be extremely difficult, if not impractical, to remove.

Air trapped in the boiler heat exchanger can be another source of noise. This can sometimes be avoided by using an eccentric reducing bush for smaller pipes attached to horizontal boiler flow tappings.

14.6 System Noise

Noise in a heating system can often be difficult to trace, especially if emanating from the circulator, since it can be transmitted and amplified along the pipework to remote parts of the installation.

Pipework noise also commonly occurs as a result of the expansion of pipework over joists or where the pipe has been left touching other pipes or a part of the building structure. Care must always be taken to ensure the pipework is correctly bracketed, is not in tension or compression and does not carry the weight of components such as the circulator. Room must be left for pipework to expand and contract without coming into contact with other pipes or the building structure. Felt pads or similar should be fitted in notches in joists where pipes will move during expansion and contraction.

14.7 Isolating Valves

A circulator should always be fitted with two isolating valves and unions to allow easy removal for maintenance purposes. These isolating valves should never be used to regulate the performance of the circulator.

14.8   Integral Circulators

A number of boilers, particularly combination and sealed system types, are supplied complete with circulators already piped and electrically wired as part of the package. In such cases the circulator is usually an important part of the operating sequence of the boiler which may also incorporate an automatic bypass valve and have an overrun requirement as part of the control function.

Boilers of this type tend to use a high proportion of the available circulator pressure to circulate water through the heat exchanger and will, for this reason, specify the pressure available to be used to circulate water through the rest of the system. Refer to the manufacturer's instructions for particular boilers to ensure that the correct temperature drop across the system is used when sizing heat emitters and pipework. If the integral circulator has insufficient capacity for the system, use a mixing header and a second circulator for radiator circuits; on no account add a second circulator in series with the integral circulator.

15.0   OPEN VENTED SYSTEMS

15.1   Feed, Expansion & Safety Pipework

Open vented systems require feed and expansion pipework correctly located relative to the circulator so that a positive system pressure is created in as much of the installation as is practical.

From the circulator around the circuit to the neutral point where the feed and expansion pipe is connected, the pressure in the pipework at any given position is the static head at that position plus the pressure created by the circulator at that position. From the neutral point around the circuit to the inlet side of the circulator, the pressure in the pipework at any given point will be the static head minus the pressure effect of the circulator.

If, particularly at high points in circuits having a low static head, the pressure effect of the circulator is to reduce pressure in the pipework, this reduction can be greater than the static head and the pressure in the pipework can then be reduced to less than the atmospheric pressure. Under these circumstances air can be induced into the pipework. This condition must be avoided. This is usually achieved by positioning the circulator in the flow pipework near the boiler and connecting the feed and expansion pipe between them.

The open safety vent pipe, sometimes incorrectly referred to as the 'expansion', must not be positioned where pressures created by the circulator could cause it to discharge water or allow air to be drawn in to the circulating pipework. Satisfactory connection schemes are shown in figs 15.1 and 15.2.

15.2   Feed & Expansion Cistern

The feed and expansion cistern is located at the highest point in the system to maintain system pressure and to supply make-up water to replace any lost due to evaporation or leaks and also to accommodate the expansion of water in the system as it heats up. As the water in the system is heated to operating temperature, its volume will increase by about 1.5%, raising the level in the feed and expansion cistern. It returns to its original level when the system cools down again. The cistern must be big enough to accommodate the expansion water without any overflowing to waste as the level rises from its cold level, which should be approximately 100mm from the base of the cistern, to its level at full temperature. BS5449 stipulates a cistern capacity of at least 5% of the total system volume. Table 15.1 gives recommended sizes for feed and expansion cisterns and pipes.

All components of the feed and expansion in contact with water should be capable of withstanding the temperature of boiling water, especially the float of the float-operated valve, which should be made of copper or a similarly heat resistant material.

	Boiler Output (kW)		
	Up to 25	25 - 45	45 - 60
Cistern nominal capacity (l)	45	70	90
Feed and expansion pipe diameter (mm)	15	22	22
Open safety vent pipe diameter (mm)	22	28	28
Overflow pipe diameter (mm)	22	28	35

TABLE 15.1: FEED & EXPANSION COMPONENTS–RECOMMENDED SIZES

15.3 Feed & Expansion Pipe

The feed and expansion (F&E) pipe connects the F&E cistern to the system and provides a route for water to expand from the system as the primary temperature rises. The pipe must have a diameter of not less than 15mm; it must not have a valve fitted in it and must not supply water for any other purpose.

An important function of the feed and expansion pipe is to quickly replenish water in the system to protect the boiler in the event of the operating thermostat failing in the open position. This will allow the burner to continue to function and generate steam, which would escape to atmosphere along the open safety vent pipe. For this reason, it is important that there are no restrictions such as motorised or manual valves along the route the feed water will take to the boiler.

15.4 Open Safety Vent Pipe

The open safety vent (OSV) pipe provides the means for air to escape from the system and a path for the relief of pressure and escape of steam in the event of boiler thermostat failure. The pipe should have the following characteristics:

- a minimum diameter of 22mm;

- it should rise continuously from its point of connection; (refer to the boiler manufacturer's instructions for the positioning of the vent in relation to the boiler – suitably designed boilers may not require a continuous rise from the boiler);

- it should contain no restrictions, such as valves; and

- it should discharge below the level of the cover of the feed and expansion cistern.

The OSV pipe should be taken from a horizontal flow pipe so that any air in the water has a better opportunity to separate. This will be improved if the flow pipe is increased by one size at a distance of approx.150/200mm before the tee, and then reduced back to normal size after the vent connection.

15.5   Pipework Arrangement

Arrangements of F&E pipework and the circulator to give positive pressure in the pipework system are shown in Figs. 15.1 and 15.2. The pipes can form part of the circulatory system providing there are no obstructions such as valves etc. between the boiler and the F & E cistern. Ensure that the specific requirements of the boiler and circulator manufacturers are observed with regard to the positioning of the F&E and OSV pipes. In fig 15.1 drawings A, B and C show layouts that have been used in low hydraulic resistance boilers in the past but are rarely adopted with modern boilers.

15.6   Close Coupled F& E and OSV Pipework

Close coupled feed and expansion and open safety vent pipes are accepted practice with most types of high and low resistance automatically controlled boilers. The connections should be made into a straight horizontal run of the flow pipe, immediately before the circulator. The distance between the connections should be no greater than 150mm to minimise the pressure differential between the feed and expansion pipe and the open safety vent pipe and, hence, to reduce the vertical movement of water in the OSV pipe. In fig 15.2 drawings D and E are used with most types of boiler. The layout shown in drawing F can only be used with a boiler having an overheat thermostat and where the boiler manufacturer approves it.

An air separator can also provide a close coupled arrangement and separate the air from the water as it enters into the unit where the velocity is reduced by the enlarged volume of the vessel. An example of this arrangement is shown in Fig 15.2E.

15.7   Combined Feed and Expansion and Open Safety Vent Pipe

A single combined F&E and OSV pipe can be fitted to boilers which incorporate an overheat thermostat in addition to the normal operating thermostat where the boiler manufacturer permits this. In this case the combined pipe is not required to account for the malfunction of the operating thermostat and need not rise directly from the boiler as shown in Fig.15.3G. Combined feed and expansion pipes (Figs. 15.3G and 15.3H) should be at least 22mm diameter.

15.8   Water Treatment

All newly installed systems need to be thoroughly internally cleansed, preferably using a cleaning fluid, after completion of the installation work. It is also necessary to add a corrosion inhibitor to the cleaned system before putting it into regular use.

This procedure must also be followed when replacement or extension work is carried out on a system.

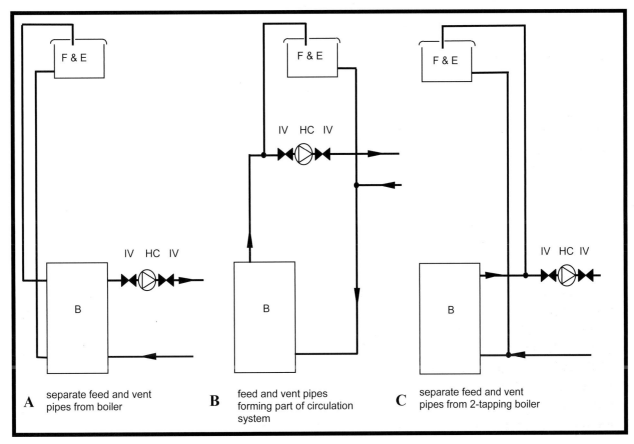

FIG 15.1 SEPARATE FEED AND EXPANSION PIPE AND OPEN SAFETY VENT PIPE CONNECTION SYSTEMS

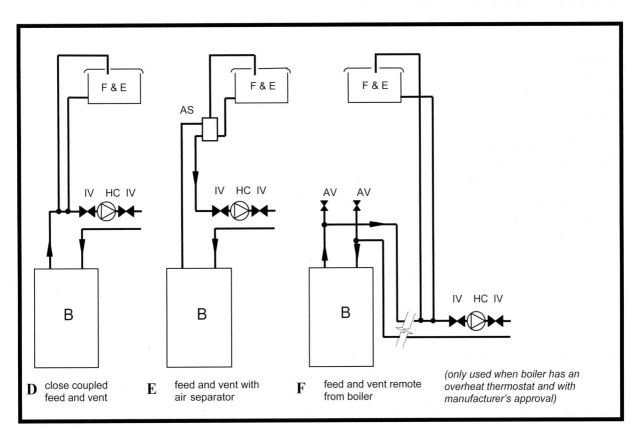

FIG 15.2   CLOSE COUPLED FEED AND EXPANSION AND OPEN SAFETY VENT PIPE CONNECTION SYSTEMS

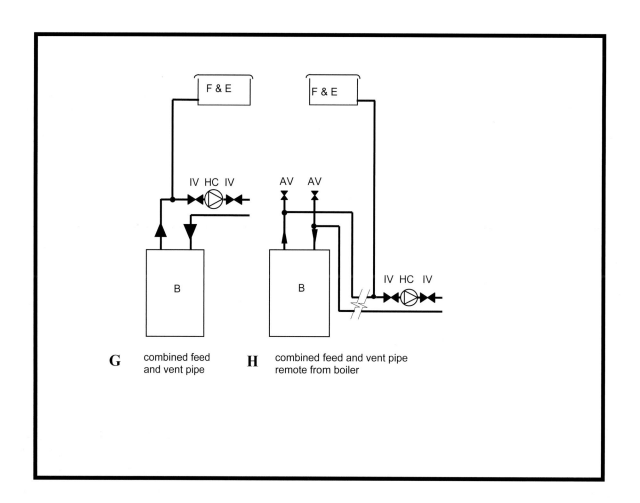

G combined feed and vent pipe

H combined feed and vent pipe remote from boiler

FIG 15.3   COMBINED FEED AND VENT PIPE ARRANGEMENTS (only to be used where a boiler has an overheat thermostat and with manufacturer's approval)

16.0 SEALED HEATING SYSTEMS

16.1 Basic Considerations

A sealed heating system eliminates the need for a feed and expansion cistern and its associated pipework, and virtually eliminates all corrosion risks since there is no possibility of ingress of air during normal operation of the system.When installed together with an unvented domestic hot water cylinder, there is no need for cisterns or pipework in the roof space. This considerably reduces the risk of frost damage and condensation in the roof space. Sealed systems are particularly advantageous in flats and bungalows where it may not be possible to obtain adequate static pressure from a cistern.

16.2 System Components

Figure 16.1 shows a typical sealed system. The system must be provided with a diaphragm expansion vessel complying with BS 4814, a pressure gauge, a means for filling, make-up and venting, and a non-adjustable safety valve. Boilers used in sealed systems should be approved for the purpose by their manufacturer and must incorporate a high limit thermostat. It is of particular importance that manufacturers' instructions are followed when installing the components of a sealed system.

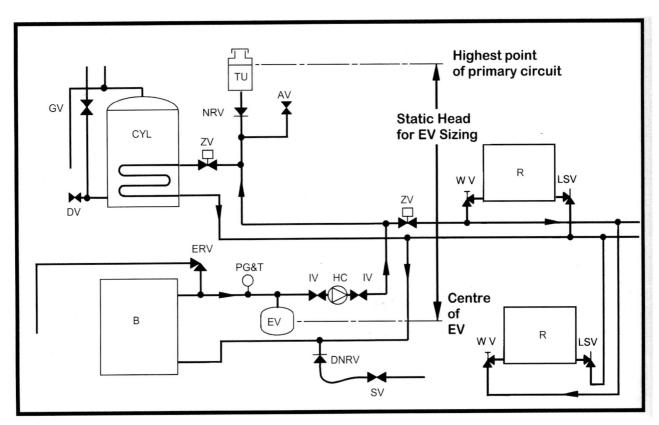

FIG 16.1   SEALED HEATING SYSTEM COMPONENTS

16.3   Expansion Vessel

The main component of a sealed heating system is the expansion vessel. It performs the same task as the feed and expansion cistern in an open vented system: to receive the increased water volume when expansion takes place as the system heats up and to maintain a positive pressure in the system. The expansion vessel contains a flexible diaphragm, which is charged on one side initially with nitrogen but is then topped up as required with air.

The expansion vessel should be located close to the suction side of the circulator to ensure that there is positive pressure in all parts of the system pipework. This will eliminate the possibility of air ingress through valve glands etc. It should be connected in such a manner as to minimise natural convection currents in order to maintain the lowest possible temperature at the diaphragm. The pipe connecting the pressure vessel to the system should have a diameter of not less than 15mm and must not contain any restriction such as an isolating valve.

It is important that the expansion vessel has sufficient acceptance volume to accommodate the expansion that would occur if the system water were heated from 10°C to 110°C. Consequently, it is important that the system volume is estimated with reasonable accuracy; a procedure for estimating system volume is shown in Section 16.12 below.

The initial charge pressure in the expansion vessel should be in accordance with manufacturers' instructions and must always exceed the static pressure of the heating system at the level of the vessel. Prior to connecting the expansion vessel to the system, the pipework should be flushed and tested. Following connection of the vessel, the system when cold should be pressurised to above the initial nitrogen pressure in the vessel (typically by 0.2 bar). This will result in a small displacement of the diaphragm as illustrated in Fig 16.2a. When the system is operational the expansion water will move into the vessel, compressing the nitrogen so that when the operating temperature is reached the system pressure will rise and the diaphragm will be displaced to accommodate the additional volume. (Fig.16.2b). BS 5449 defines the practical acceptance volume of the vessel as what it will accept when the gauge pressure rises to 0.35 bar below the safety valve setting.

If the initial system water pressure is too high or the nitrogen fill pressure in the vessel is too low, the diaphragm will be displaced too far into the vessel, which will then be unable to accommodate the volume of expansion water. This will result in an increase in the system pressure and the safety valve will lift.

16.4   Safety (Pressure Relief) Valve

All sealed systems must have a non-adjustable safety valve set to lift at a gauge pressure not exceeding 3 bar (300 kPa). Safety valves must also have a manual testing device, valve seating materials that will prevent sticking in a closed position and provision for connecting a full bore discharge pipe. The valve should be connected to the flow pipe close to the boiler with a metal discharge pipe installed to an open tundish, which should then discharge in a safe visible external low level location. No valves should be fitted between the safety valve and the heat exchanger.

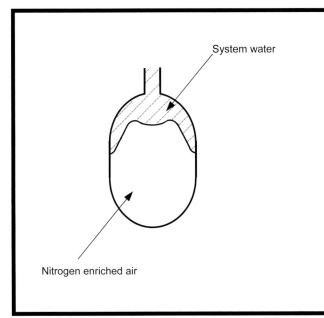

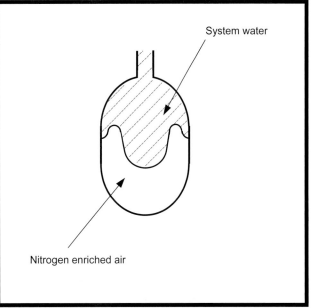

FIG 16.2a EXPANSION VESSEL (COLD)

FIG 16.2b EXPANSION VESSEL (HOT)

16.5   Pressure Gauge & Thermometer

A pressure gauge is provided so that the pressure may be checked and the system charged to the correct pressure when commissioning or topping up. The pressure gauge must be readable from the system filling position. A thermometer, which may be combined with the pressure gauge, shows the temperature of the flow water from the boiler. Care should be taken to ensure that the thermometer is fitted to the boiler or the flow pipe, not to a non-circulating pipe, and that the thermometer pocket does not restrict the bore of the pipework.

16.6   Filling Loop

Filling and pressurising the system is normally achieved by a direct connection from the cold water supply main through a special filling loop. This is an arrangement of fittings which incorporates a BS 1010 stop valve, double check valve with test point, and a flexible pipe which should be disconnected and removed after use and protective caps fitted over the ends of the stop and check valves.

16.7   Water Top-Up

Sealed systems do not lose water due to evaporation and so, provided there are no leaks, make up water should not usually required except during the initial period of operation when air in the fill water is being removed from the system.

Lost water can be replaced by any of the following methods.

1. Refilling and pressurising manually through the filling loop.

2. Refilling automatically through a top-up unit.

3. Refilling automatically through a make-up cistern.

16.8   Top-Up Unit

The top-up unit is connected to the highest part of the system and is fitted with a double check valve assembly and automatic air eliminator. The unit, which has a water capacity of about three litres, is topped up manually when the water level drops. It is also useful as an indicator of leaks in the system. It should be connected either to the return side of the radiator distribution pipework or to the return side of the primary domestic hot water circuit.

The commissioning of a system is greatly simplified when a top-up unit is installed as initial pressurisation is unnecessary.

16.9   Make-up Cistern

The installation of a make-up cistern for filling and make-up water should be considered for larger installations. This is typically a conventional 45 litre plastic cistern with lid, overflow and ball valve connected to the mains water supply.

The cistern should be sited at least 300mm above the highest point of the system and the outlet fitted with a double check valve assembly and a stop valve. The cistern must not be used for any other purpose. The filling of the system will be simplified but the main advantage of a manual top-up unit, that of knowing water is being lost, will not be available because of the automatic replenishment of water.

16.10 Automatic Air Eliminator

Provision must be made for venting air from sealed systems, using either automatic or manual air vents. Automatic air vents should be fitted at the highest points of the system and should be float operated. Hygroscopic types of automatic air vent should not be used because they allow continuous evaporation of small quantities of water. The automatic vent incorporated into some boilers is sufficient when combined with a manual air vent fitted at the highest point in the system. Automatic air vents can be obtained with an integral shut-off valve, which allows cleaning to be carried out without draining down the system.

An air separator with an automatic air eliminator is an optional item to be considered on larger domestic systems to assist commissioning and for the easy removal of air. It is usually fitted on the flow pipe between the boiler and the circulator.

16.11 Sealed System Boilers

Boilers with sealed system components already fitted within the casing, or with casing extensions to hide the components from view, are readily available and provide a compact alternative to installing separate components.

16.12 Expansion Vessel Sizing

The expansion vessel must be sized according to the total volume of the water in the system, using Worksheet Eight – Water Content of System, which is shown on page 81.

The water content of boilers and other principal components is available from manufacturers' data sheets. Radiator manufacturers usually show water content in terms of section or unit length. However, hot water cylinder manufacturers usually only publish the surface area of the heating coils in cylinders. Table 16.1 gives estimated water content of the primary coils of various sizes of cylinder, which may be used where no other information is available from manufacturers. For pipework, use Table 16.2 estimate water content.

Use Table 16.3 to find the minimum expansion vessel capacity from the total system volume calculated with Worksheet Eight.

Cylinder capacity (litres)	Water content of Primary heating coil (litres)
96	1.7
125	2.3
145	2.7
175	3.2
225	4.1

TABLE 16.1 WATER CONTENT OF HOT WATER CYLINDER HEATING COILS

Nominal pipe size (mm)	Water content per metre (litres)
8	0.036
10	0.055
15	0.145
22	0.320
28	0.539
35	0.835
42	1.232

TABLE 16.2 WATER CONTENT OF COPPER TUBES

Safety valve setting (bar)	3.0			2.5			2.0	
Vessel charge and initial system pressure (bar)	0.5	1.0	1.5	0.5	1.0	1.5	0.5	1.0
Total water content of system (litres)	Select an Expansion Vessel with a nominal volume not less than that given below (litres)							
25	2.1	2.7	3.9	2.3	3.3	5.9	2.8	5.0
50	4.2	5.4	7.8	4.7	6.7	11.8	5.6	10.0
75	6.3	8.2	11.7	7.0	10.0	17.7	8.4	15.0
100	8.3	10.9	15.6	9.4	13.4	23.7	11.3	20.0
125	10.4	13.6	19.5	11.7	16.7	29.6	14.1	25.0
150	12.5	16.3	23.4	14.1	20.1	35.5	16.9	30.0
175	14.6	19.1	27.3	16.4	23.4	41.4	19.7	35.0
200	16.7	21.8	31.2	18.8	26.8	47.4	22.6	40.0
225	18.7	24.5	35.1	21.1	30.1	53.3	25.4	45.0
250	20.8	27.2	39.0	23.5	33.5	59.2	28.2	50.0
275	22.9	30.0	42.9	25.8	36.8	65.1	31.0	55.0
300	25.0	32.7	46.8	28.2	40.2	71.1	33.9	60.0
Multiplying factors for other system volumes	0.0833	0.109	0.156	0.094	0.134	0.237	0.113	0.2

TABLE 16.3   CAPACITIES OF EXPANSION VESSELS

16.13   Water Treatment

All newly installed systems need to be thoroughly cleansed, preferably using a cleaning fluid, after completion of the installation work. It is also necessary to add a corrosion inhibitor to the cleaned system before putting it into regular use.

This procedure must also be followed when replacement or extension work is carried out on a system.

DOMESTIC HEATING DESIGN GUIDE
WORKSHEET EIGHT – WATER CONTENT OF SYSTEM

Component					Water content litres
Boiler	Manufacturer and type	Output kW	Water content *(from manufacturer's literature)* Enter in end column		
	117F	15			0.60
Cylinder	Manufacturer and type	Size litres	Water content of coil *(from manufacturer's literature)* Enter in end column		
	Unvented (coil)	120			2.10
Pipework	Diameter mm	Length m	Water content per metre litres		
	8	20	0.036		0.72
	10	15	0.055		0.83
	15	30	0.145		4.35
	22	12	0.320		3.84
	28	—	0.539		—
	35	—	0.835		—
	42	—	1.232		—
Heat emitters	Location	Type (SP,DP DPC, etc.)	Height mm	No. of sections or length	Water content per section or length *(from manufacturer's literature)* litres	
	Lounge	SP	600	26	0.30	7.80
	Kitchen/dining	DP	600	19	0.60	11.40
	Hall	DP	600	13	0.60	7.80
	Bathroom	SP	600	13	0.30	3.90
	Bedroom 1	SP	600	22	0.26	5.72
	Bedroom 2	SP	600	16	0.26	4.16
					Total system water content	53.22

EXPANSION VESSEL SELECTION

Static pressure of water above expansion vessel (cold)	Total system water content	Safety valve setting	Vessel selected *(from manufacturer's catalogue)*	
			Vessel charge and initial system fill pressure	Vessel volume
bar	litres	bar	bar	litres
0.3	53.22	3.0	0.5	8

17.0 PIPEWORK INSULATION

17.1 Regulations

Building regulations require that heating pipes should be insulated unless their heat loss contributes to the useful heating requirement of a room or space. Water regulations require that pipes and fittings in an unheated area shall, as far as is reasonably practical, be protected against damage from freezing and other causes.

17.2 Insulation of Heating System Pipework

Pipes should be insulated unless they contribute to the useful heat requirement of a heated room or space. The thickness of insulation required by building regulations is equal to the outside diameter of the pipe (up to a maximum of 40mm) provided that the thermal conductivity of the insulation material does not exceed 0.045 W/ (mK).

The hot pipes connected to hot water storage vessels including the open safety vent pipe and the primary flow and return to the heat exchanger, should be insulated for at least one metre from their points of connection or to the point at which they become concealed. The insulation should be not less than 15mm of a material having a thermal conductivity of 0.045 W/ (mK) or equivalent.

Transfer of heat between hot pipes and cold pipes should be avoided where possible by maintaining adequate separation between them. Where hot and cold pipes have to be run adjacent to each other, they should be insulated to minimise heat transfer.

17.3 Insulation in Unheated Areas

Insulation is required by water regulations to reduce the likelihood of frost damage to pipes and fittings, including cold water service pipes and heating system pipes. This applies to all cold water fittings located within the building but outside the thermal envelope, and to those outside the building.

Where low temperatures persist insulation will only delay the onset of freezing. Its efficiency is dependent upon its thickness and thermal conductivity in relation to the size of pipe, the time of exposure, the location and possibly the wind-chill factor. The thickness of insulation is designed to provide protection for a period of up to 12 hours. Where protection is required for longer periods, or the premises are left unoccupied, this should be provided by a frost thermostat set to activate the heating system when the air temperature drops to a pre-selected level or by draining down. Self-regulating trace heating conforming to BS 6351, in conjunction with a nominal thickness of thermal insulation, is also an acceptable method of protection against freezing.

Changes to Part L of the Building Regulations introduced April 2005

Changes to Part L of the Building Regulations came into effect on the 1st of April 2005, raising performance standards for central heating boilers. The "poorest acceptable" SEDBUK efficiency has been raised to 86% for boilers fired by mains gas and LPG, to 85% for regular oil-fired boilers, and to 82% (as calculated by the SAP 2001 method) for oil-fired combination boilers. This will require the fitting of condensing boilers when the fuel is mains gas or LPG.

The changes are set out a document entitled *Approved Document L1: Conservation of fuel and power in dwellings - Amended 2005*. They apply to all new dwellings and to existing dwellings when boilers are installed or replaced. It is recognised, however, that it may not always be reasonable to fit a condensing boiler in existing dwellings, because of difficulties in finding a suitable flue location or means of condensate disposal. The amendment includes a new *Appendix G: Assessing the case for a non-condensing boiler*, which contains a points based assessment procedure and a declaration form to be completed by the installer and retained by the householder.

Two documents providing additional information about the changes are also available from the Building Regulations Division of the Office of the Deputy Prime Minister (ODPM). A *Guide to the Condensing Boiler Installation Procedure for Dwellings* has been written to help heating installers carry out a condensing boiler installation assessment using the procedure as set out in Appendix G to Approved Document L1. The information leaflet *Gas and oil central-heating boilers - Advice to householders* has also been produced.

All three documents referred to above may be downloaded without charge from the ODPM website www.odpm.gov.uk. The relevant files may be found by following the path: Home > Building Regulations > Building Regulations – Documents and Publications > Conservation of Fuel and Power (Part L).

The changes to Part L described above are part of a wider programme of revisions that is currently in progress and expected to come into effect at the end of December 2005. The Domestic Heating Design Guide will be revised accordingly when the full details of the revisions are published later in the year.

CIBSE Domestic Building Services Panel

9/4/05

Thermal insulating materials should be of the closed cell type complying with BS 5422 and be installed in accordance with BS 5970. Insulation should be neatly fitted with formed mitred joints at elbows and tees and should cover all valves and fittings. The manufacturer's approved adhesives should be used on all butt and seam joints.

Hot water fittings outside the thermal envelope, where water is likely to be static for a period, should be protected against freezing. The thickness of insulation applied to hot water pipes for energy conservation purposes is usually of insufficient thickness to protect against low temperature conditions. (see Section 17.2)

For cold water services two conditions are identified:
'Normal conditions' – unheated rooms within the thermal envelope of the heated accommodation, such as store rooms or roof spaces below the roof insulation.
'Extreme conditions' – outside the normal heated envelope of the building, such as roof spaces above the roof insulation.

Typical insulation thicknesses to manufacturers' recommendations are shown in Table 17.1.

External diameter of pipe (mm)	Within the insulated envelope of the dwelling (mm)	Outside the insulated envelope of the dwelling (mm)
15	25	32
22	19	25
28	19	19
35	13	13

TABLE 17.1: THICKNESS OF INSULATION FOR COLD WATER PIPES TO PREVENT FREEZING

18.0 SYSTEM CONTROLS

18.1 Control Selection

If the procedures described in this Guide are followed, they should result in a system that is capable of heating the dwelling under design conditions. However, most of the time much less heat output is required. Controls are needed to ensure that the desired temperatures are achieved in each room, as and when required, under all conditions, including those when little or no additional heat is required.

The selection of appropriate controls also plays a key part in the overall running costs of a heating or hot water system. The cost benefits of controls should not be underestimated since upgrading controls on older heating systems can save up to 15% on energy bills.

18.2 Control Components

Table 18.1a lists common components used in central heating systems and gives a brief description of their functions. Table 18.1b lists additional control functions that may be carried out by additional circuitry built into one or more of the control components or, in the case of boiler interlock, simply by the way in which the components are interconnected. For example, optimum start may be built into the unit that also carries out the functions of the programmer. Such multifunction units are often given names such as "boiler energy managers". Appendix B gives more detailed definitions of control components.

CONTROL TYPE	PURPOSE and BENEFITS
Timeswitch	Simple time control of a system or part of a system.
Programmer	Combination including two clock-operated switches so that space heating and hot water can be controlled independently.
Room Thermostat*	Simple low cost room temperature control
Programmable room thermostat*	Allows temperature to be set for different periods in the day or week. Provides energy saving and convenient control. Important if occupancy is varied over the day or week. Provides a "night setback feature" where a minimum temperature can be maintained at night.
DHW cylinder thermostat	Simple control for temperature domestic hot water cylinder.
Frost thermostat or low-limit thermostat	Simple override control, used to avoid frost damage to dwelling, boiler and system.

TABLE 18.1a: CONTROL COMPONENTS USED IN CENTRAL HEATING SYSTEMS

* Wireless units provide increased positional flexibility. They should carry the "RadioMark" or equivalent to avoid signal interference.

CONTROL TYPE	PURPOSE and BENEFITS
Pipe thermostat	Used with frost thermostat to avoid unnecessary boiler operation in cold weather and so reduce running costs.
Thermostatic radiator valve	Used to limit temperatures in individual rooms. Reduces energy consumption where there are incidental gains and solar gain.
Motorized valve	2-port or 3-port valve used in conjunction with room and DHW cylinder thermostats to control water flow from boiler to heating and hot water circuits. Can be used to provide zone control e.g. separate time and/or central heating temperature control in sleeping area.
"Boiler Interlock"	NOT a control but a wiring arrangement to stop the boiler firing when there is no demand for heat.
Automatic bypass valve	It ensures a minimum flow through the boiler but also reduces the likelihood of excessive noise in the radiator system.

TABLE 18.1b: CONTROL COMPONENTS USED IN CENTRAL HEATING SYSTEMS

CONTROL FUNCTIONS	PURPOSE AND BENEFITS
Compensator	Reduces boiler water temperature for space heating according to internal/external air temperature and will increase the efficiency of condensing boilers
Delayed start	Reduces energy use by delaying boiler start time when weather is mild
Optimum start	Adjusts the heating start time to give the required dwelling comfort temperature at a chosen time
Temperature setback or night setback	Allows a reduced temperature to be maintained at certain times, for example at night. Reduces the risk of condensation and improves comfort by reducing dwelling warm up time
Narrow temperature differential	Reduces the temperature "swing" between a boiler switching on and off and so increases comfort. May save energy consumption by reducing "set" temperature
Self-learning	Reduces appliance "on" time by taking account of previous characteristics
Anti-cycling control	Delays boiler firing to reduce cycling frequency but unlikely to provide significant savings

TABLE 18.2 ADDITIONAL CONTROL FUNCTIONS

Recommended minimum control packages are shown below.

<u>All</u> wet systems must have:-

- Boiler interlock, i.e. a wiring arrangement such that the boiler cannot fire unless there is a demand from either space heating or hot water;

- Thermostatic radiator valves fitted to all radiators except in rooms where a controlling room thermostat (standard or programmable) is fitted;

- Frost protection where necessary to protect the appliance, system and dwelling.

In addition the following types of system must have:-

EXISTING SEMI GRAVITY SYSTEMS

NOTE: When upgrading it is preferable to convert systems to fully-pumped operation but where this is impractical the following should be adopted. (New systems must always be fully pumped.)

- Two channel programmer

- Room thermostat

- Cylinder thermostat

- One 2-port motorized valve[1] fitted on the gravity circuit to the hot water cylinder

- Check valve to prevent gravity circulation in the radiator circuit

Alternatively, the functions of the programmer can be carried out by programmable room and cylinder thermostats.

FULLY PUMPED – *One heating zone system*

- Two channel programmer

- Room thermostat

- Cylinder thermostat

- One 3-port motorized valve or two 2-port motorized valves for pumped space and water heating

- An automatic bypass valve should be fitted (except where one is incorporated into the boiler).

---

[1] Motorized valves in gravity primary circuits must be fitted so that their operation does not interfere with the route of the OSV or F&E pipes to the boiler. In order that Boiler Interlock may be achieved, the motorized valve actuator must have a SPDT auxiliary switch.

FULLY PUMPED – *Two heating zone system*

- Three-channel programmer.

- Two room thermostats (for two separate heating zones).

- Cylinder thermostat

- Three 2-port motorized valves for pumped heating to two heating zones and the hot water zone.

- An automatic bypass valve should be fitted (except where one is incorporated into the boiler).

Alternatively, the functions of the three channel programmer can be carried out separately, for example by using two programmable room thermostats and a programmable cylinder thermostat.

COMBINATION BOILER SYSTEMS

- Single channel timeswitch/programmer

- Room thermostat

- An automatic bypass valve should be fitted (except where one is incorporated into the boiler).

Alternatively, the timeswitch/programmer can be omitted if a programmable room thermostat is used.

18.4 Enhanced Control Functions

Additional benefits in convenience, comfort and energy consumption can be obtained by using some of the functions described in Table 18.1 above. **Weather compensation** reduces average boiler water temperature in mild weather; this is particularly beneficial where condensing boilers are used because it reduces the return water temperature and increases the proportion of time the boiler operates in condensing mode. **Delayed start** can reduce boiler firing by delaying start-up in milder weather. **Optimum start** will also reduce boiler firing when it is not required but can advance as well as delay start-up. Both types of control can save energy and/or enhance comfort depending on how they are set up. **Narrow temperature differential thermostats** reduce the temperature "swing" between demand and satisfaction at the thermostat and hence the variation in room temperature. This should have the effect of marginally reducing the average temperature at which room needs to be maintained to achieve comfort, assuming that the thermostat is set on the minimum temperature maintained.

18.5 Typical Control Arrangements

Some of the more popular control arrangements are described on the following pages. By-passes have not been shown on the main diagrams which follow; they are described separately in section 18.6 and should be provided where necessary.

Product considerations should include reliability, ease of servicing, future availability of spare parts, operating efficiency and ease of use. Control systems are often sold as packages containing all the necessary components and instructions for their use in common system layouts.

18.6 By-Pass Arrangements

The need for a by-pass depends on the boiler and the control system. Some boilers require circulator overrun to dissipate heat when the boiler is switched off. Controls may also shut down or restrict flow while the circulator is still operating, especially in systems using TRVs and 2-port valves. In each case, a by-pass is needed to provide a circulation path.

Where a low water content boiler is used, a permanent by-pass must be fitted directly after the circulator between the main flow and return pipes. Refer to manufacturer's instructions for particular boilers, including sizing. A minimum of 15mm diameter pipe is typically required for boilers up to 19kW output and 22mm on larger sizes. A manual by-pass should be fitted with a lock-shield valve, which must be regulated to provide the minimum flow rate specified for the boiler. (see Figure 18.1)

Alternatively, an automatic by-pass valve may be used, particularly with thermostatic radiator valves or zone valves, (see Figure 18.2). This type of valve is set when the system is commissioned so that under normal working conditions it is either closed or partly open, depending on the application. In operation, it opens when pressure increases in response to reduced flow through the circuit.

The minimum flow rate of water required through the boiler by-pass when all other circuits are closed is specified by the boiler manufacturer, probably in terms of the temperature drop across the boiler. The actual flow rate can vary between 10 l/min (0.17kg/s) and 40 l/min (0.67kg/s). The flow rate through the bypass will however reduce when the heating circuits are fully open. For the purpose of estimating the total flow rate the flow rate can be assumed to be 0.10kg/s for a 15mm pipe and 0.25kg/s for a 22mm pipe.

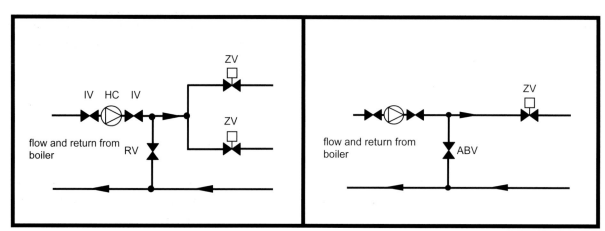

FIG 18.1 MANUAL BY-PASS ARRANGEMENTS   **FIG 18.2 AUTOMATIC BY-PASS ARRANGEMENTS**

18.7 Three-Way Control Valves

Fig 18.3 shows a typical fully pumped system with a mid-position motorised valve which will provide water to the heating system and/or domestic hot water cylinder when one or both operating thermostats call for heat.

The same pipework layout may be used with a diverter valve, which directs all of the flow from the boiler to either the heating system or the domestic hot water cylinder on a priority basis. Priority is usually assigned to the domestic hot water, which will heat to the cylinder thermostat setting before the heating circuit will be allowed to operate.

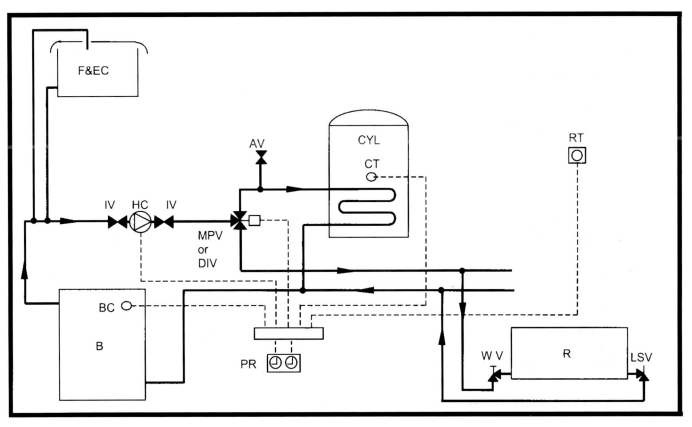

FIG 18.3   HEATING AND DOMESTIC HOT WATER USING A MID-POSITION OR DIVERTER VALVE

18.8 Two Separate Zone Valves

A very commonly used layout as shown in Figure 18.4 where one two port motorised valve controls the Domestic Hot Water and another one controls the space heating circuit. Cylinder and room thermostats control the valves in addition to separate timing control. Thermostatic radiator valves are very often fitted in addition.

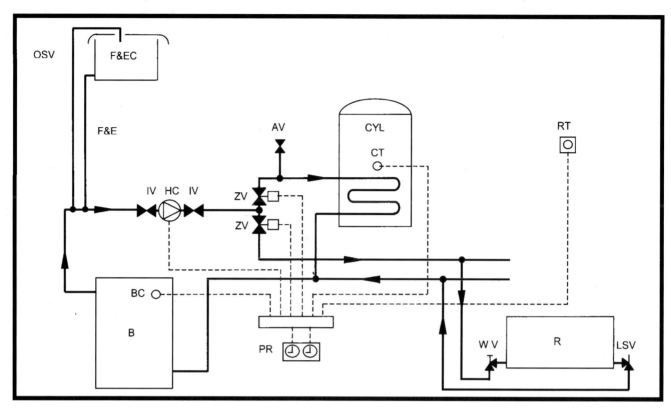

FIG 18.4   HEATING AND DOMESTIC HOT WATER USING TWO ZONE VALVES

18.9   Additional Zone Control

For larger houses, or where separate parts of a house are used at varying times, it is advantageous to provide more than one controlled circuit for the space heating.[1] This is normally achieved by serving the separate area through an additional space heating circuit controlled by a motorised valve, as is shown in Figure 18.5. To meet more extensive control requirements it is possible to add several separate circuits in this manner, with each given its own time and temperature control.

[1]In England and Wales no space heating zone is permitted to control an area with a floor area larger than 150m². (See Approved Document L1 to the Building Regulations)

18.10   Primary Circuit Radiator

The facility to use a radiator, towel rail or ladder rail in a bathroom or a separate heating coil in a cupboard after the main heating system has been turned off for the summer can be incorporated into the system layouts in Figs. 18.3, 18.4 or 18.5.

The pipework arrangement required is shown in Fig.18.6, and includes a thermostatic radiator valve. The radiator will operate whenever the cylinder thermostat or the heating room thermostat calls for heat.

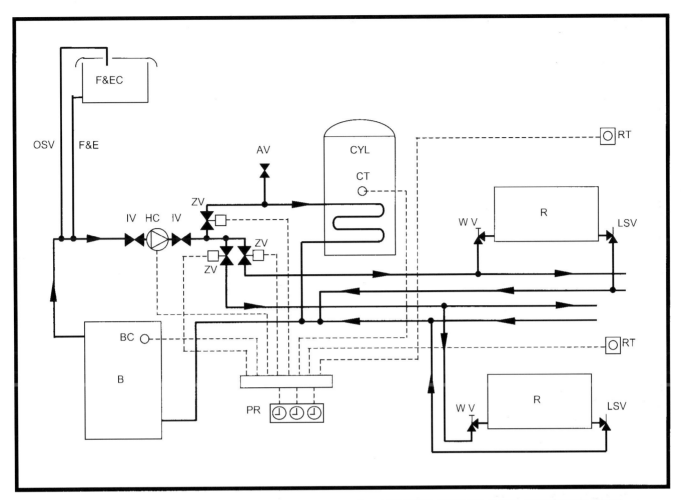

FIG 18.5   HEATING AND DOMESTIC HOT WATER WITH ONE ZONE VALVE FOR HOT WATER AND 2 ZONE VALVES FOR HEATING CIRCUITS

18.11 Compensating Controls

The two pipe system can be used to serve all types of emitters; radiators, natural convectors, fan convectors, skirting heating, underfloor coils and warm air heater batteries. However, care must be taken when designing pipe layouts and using advanced control systems such as temperature compensating mixing valves that different types of emitter, (e.g., radiators and underfloor coils), are not included in the same circuit.

A mixed temperature water circuit must not be used to serve fan convectors or warm air heater batteries as both these items require maximum boiler water temperature to produce an acceptable output air temperature. Also, radiators should not be fitted to an underfloor coil heating circuit, which will have been designed to work on a low flow temperature.

The boiler heat output of a modulating system is achieved by electronic direct-on-burner control. This receives signals from internal and external temperature sensors, which enable the controller to evaluate how much heat is required for space heating whilst also giving priority to domestic hot water production.

The flow temperature is constantly checked by the controller and adjusted for any variations of external and internal air temperature. Some controllers will also optimise the start time of the system through a self learning process of recalling previous data and relating it to present conditions so that the property will reach the desired comfort level at the occupancy time and not before.

A fully compensated system which provides maximum energy saving and comfort is illustrated in Fig. 18.7. Depending on the type of boiler to be used, an automatic by-pass valve may also be required. This should be fitted between the flow and return to the cylinder with the primary circulator wired electrically so that it would respond to any overrun requirement made by the boiler.

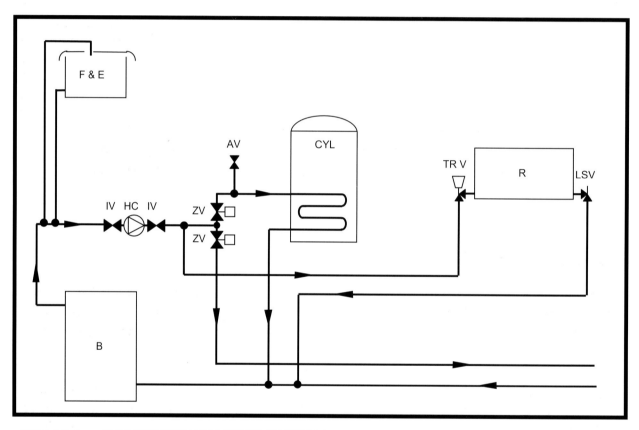

FIG 18.6   DOMESTIC HEATING SYSTEM LAYOUT SHOWING CONNECTIONS FOR THE BATHROOM RADIATOR TO OPERATE IN SUMMER AND WINTER

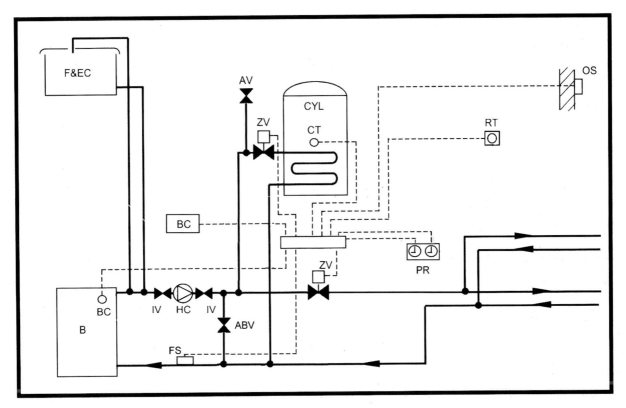

FIG 18.7   FULLY COMPENSATED HEATING SYSTEM WITH OUTSIDE AND INSIDE TEMPERATURE DETECTORS AND DOMESTIC HOT WATER CONTROLS

18.12 Linked Fuel Control

A solid fuel appliance with a water heating capability can be linked into a fully pumped system which has an automatically controlled boiler served by gas or oil, so that either one or both boilers can be used as the heat source. The solid fuel appliance can be an open fire, a conventional boiler, multifuel stove or cooker.

Figure 18.8 shows the recommended layout for a system in which a solid fuel appliance is linked to a gas or oil boiler. The solid fuel appliance heats some radiators, typically in the centre of the house; the automatic (oil or gas) boiler heats the other radiators, which are fitted with thermostatic radiator valves. Heat is provided to the domestic hot water using separate coils in a twin-coil cylinder or a by fitting an immersion coil in the immersion heater boss of a single coil cylinder. The coil connected to the automatic boiler is controlled in the normal manner by a cylinder thermostat.

This arrangement ensures that there is no exchange or mixing of the primary circuit water between the two systems. It operates by using the automatic boiler to provide the additional heat required to supplement that supplied by the solid fuel boiler and, at the same time to provide good control of the system.

In all cases, dual fuel systems of this type should be designed and operated in compliance with the instructions of the manufacturers of both heating appliances.

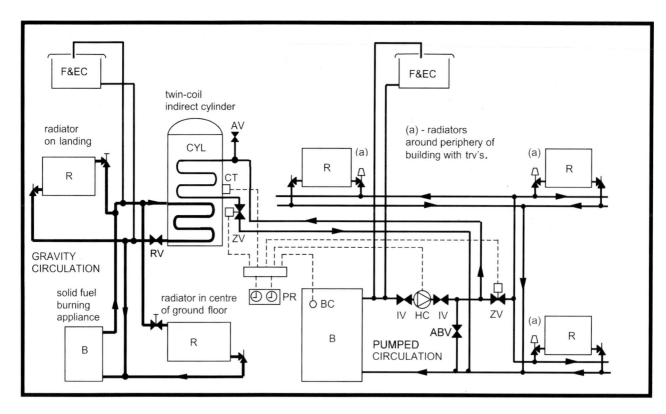

FIG 18.8   LINKED FUEL SYSTEM INCORPORATING A SOLID FUEL BURNING APPLIANCE AND EITHER A GAS OR OIL-FIRED BOILER

19.0 COMBUSTION AIR, VENTILATION AND FLUES

19.1 Air Supply Requirements

Heating appliances require a supply of air for combustion and for cooling. Specific requirements for air supply relating to heating appliances aim to ensure:

- sufficient air for proper combustion, flue operation and cooling;

- that no hazards to health arise for combustion products; and

- that no damage occurs to the fabric of the building through heat or fire.

Requirements relating to combustion air apply to open (or conventionally) flued appliances, which draw their combustion air from the rooms in which they are installed, but not to room-sealed appliances, which draw their supply directly from outside. Permanent air vents are required, sized according to the type and gross heat input of gas appliances and the heat output of oil-fired boilers. In addition, for all types of appliance, it is necessary to comply with any special requirements stated by their manufacturers.

A compartment containing an appliance must have purpose-designed vents at low and high level. The vents must be non-closable and at least large enough to admit all of the air required by the appliance for combustion and ventilation, whether the enclosure draws its air from a room or directly from outside. Appliances in compartments need cooling ventilation air to circulate around them, whether they are open-flued or room sealed. It is also possible to install an open flued appliance in a **balanced compartment** which is sealed from the remainder of the building and whose ventilation is so arranged in conjunction with the appliance flue as to achieve a balanced flue effect.

Requirements for gas appliances are given in the relevant parts of *Gas Safety (Installation and Use) Regulations* and BS 5440: Part 2: 2000.

Requirements for oil-fired appliances are given in BS 5410: Part 1: 1997

In all cases, refer to manufacturers' instructions for additional requirements applying to particular equipment.

19.2 Interaction of Extract Ventilation and Open-Flued Appliances

If the pressure in a room containing an open flued appliance is lowered by mechanical extract ventilation, flue gases may be drawn into the room from the appliance. This can happen even when the extraction is not from the same room that contains the appliance, and may be aggravated by fans in equipment such as tumble driers. Flue gases can cause hazardous levels

95

of carbon monoxide. Where open flued appliances are to be installed in areas affected mechanical extractor fans, the following precautions should be observed.

- For gas appliances: where the appliance and the extract fan are located in a kitchen, follow the spillage test procedure set out in the relevant appendix to BS 5440: Part 1: 2000.

- For oil appliances: comply with the recommendation in OFTEC Technical Information Note TI/112.

- Extract ventilation should not be installed in the same room as a solid fuel appliance. Further guidance may be obtained from BRE Information Paper IP 7/94 and from the Heating Equipment Testing and Advisory Service.

19.3 Flues

All combustion appliances must:

- be so installed that there is an adequate supply of air to them for combustion and for the efficient working of any flue pipe or chimney;

- have adequate provision for the discharge of the products of combustion to the outside air;

- be so installed, with fireplaces, flues and chimneys so constructed, as to minimise the risk of the building catching fire as a result of their use.

The second and third of those requirements relate specifically to flues.

For gas fired appliances, guidance is given in the *Gas Safety (Installation and Use) Regulations*. Some important points include:

- any appliance in a bath or shower room must be of the room-sealed type;

- a gas fire or other gas space heater of more than 14kW must not be installed in a room intended for sleeping accommodation unless the appliance is room sealed;

- LPG fired appliances should not be installed in basements.

The Regulations also cover:

- the positioning of flues in relation of boundaries and openings;

- protection from heat for persons likely to come into contact with flues;

- the diameter of flues required for different types of appliances;

- materials from which flues chimneys may be constructed and how chimneys may be lined to serve gas fired appliances.

Flues for oil fired appliances should meet the requirements set out in BS 5410: Part 1:1997.

- masonry chimneys must be lined. Liners should not be oversized.

- Any appliance in a bath or shower room or bedroom must be of the room-sealed type.

19.4 SE-Ducts and U-Ducts

A SE-duct is a single rising duct built in to a large multi-occupation building to which a number of appliances are connected. It has an opening at the bottom to provide fresh air for the appliances and an opening at the top to provide an outlet for combustion products. A U-duct is a pair of rising ducts joined at their base and open at the top, one to provide fresh air and the other to provide an outlet for combustion products. Only room-sealed appliances may be connected to SE-ducts and U-ducts and connection should be made in compliance with guidance obtained from the manufacturers of the appliances.

20.0 FUEL STORAGE

20.1 Oil Storage

The installation of oil storage and supply pipes is covered by building regulations and by environmental legislation.

The following points should be considered.

- **Quantity to be stored.** Larger storage capacity reduces the number of deliveries and fuel cost. For domestic use 2500 litres is recommended if there is space.

- **Fire protection.** If the tank is closer than 1.8 metres to a building or 760 mm to a boundary, some simple fire protection measures are required. All tanks must be installed over a fireproof base. Dimensions and other details are given in BS5410 Part 1: 1997. OFTEC Technical Information Note TI/131 also covers the subject.

- **Environmental protection.** Domestic oil tanks up to 2500 litres capacity do not have to be bunded unless their installation fails the risk assessment in OFTEC Technical Information Note TI/133. The TI/133 risk assessment must be completed for every tank installation.

- **Tank construction.** Steel tanks should comply with OFS T200. Plastic tanks should comply with OFS Tl00.

- **Oil supply pipes.** Oil supply pipes must be installed in accordance with the requirements of BS 5410:Part1:1997; remote acting fire valves to OFS E101 are required for all installations. Underground pipework should comply with OFTEC Technical Information Note TI/134.

- **Tank location.** Storage tanks should be located on firm foundations in accordance with BS 5410:Part 1:1997, with good access for delivery, inspection and maintenance. Further guidance on location is given in OFTEC Technical Book 3.

- **Tank gauges.** Oil storage tanks must be provided with an easily readable gauge, either mounted on the tank or remotely located in a convenient position. Gauges should comply with OFS E103.

20.2 LPG Storage

LPG installations are controlled by the Gas Safety (Installation and Use) Regulations. LPG storage facilities, including cylinders and bulk storage tanks, should comply with the guidance set out in COP 1.

Building regulations also give guidance that, if followed, would normally ensure compliance with the Gas Safety (Installation and Use) Regulations. LPG tanks should be adequately separated from buildings, the boundary of the property, any fixed sources of ignition and from one another. The guidance also specifies acceptable forms of barrier to place between tanks and the items to be separated from them and minimum separation distances for different tank capacities with and without barriers.

Recommended LPG storage tank capacities are listed in Table 20.1 Tanks must be accessible for fuel deliveries, usually not more than 25 metres from the delivery tanker position.

Boiler output kW	Minimum storage (litres)
Up to 15	360
15 to 25	1200
25 to 45	1800

TABLE 20.1: RECOMMENDED LPG STORAGE CAPACITY

21.0 THE SPECIFICATION

21.1 The Quotation

Quotations, whether for a new heating installation, an extension to an existing system or a replacement system, should give information about the design and the materials to be used and should be fully detailed so that the customer has no doubt about the work included. The price and conditions of trading should be stated, together with a full description of the work to be undertaken.

Any additional work necessary to enable the installation to be carried out or the system operate, but which has not been included in the quotation should also be clearly stated.

The following list is the minimum technical information to be included in a specification.

21.2 Design Conditions and Temperatures

External Temperature	°C
Heating flow temperature	°C
List of rooms to be heated	
Temperatures to be achieved in every room	°C

Number of air changes per hour in every room

21.3 Incoming and Existing Services

Comment on the adequacy of existing services, or any improvements required to make them adequate.

21.4 Heat Generators

Location of boiler etc.
Make and type
Heat output kW
If a combination boiler, state the hot water flow rate in litres/minute and temperature rise in degrees C

21.5 Boiler Flue and Chimney

Type of flue - conventional or room-sealed
Terminal position and type
Terminal guard
Flue liner and size
New or existing flue

21.6 Fuel Storage

(Oil or LPG installations)
Size of tank and construction
Location
Filling position
Insurance details (LPG)

21.7 Ventilation

Type and location of air vents for combustion air and ventilation.

21.8 Heat Emitters

Make and type
Paint finish - primer or gloss
Location - room and position

21.9 Heat Emitter Controls

Make and type

21.10 Hot Water Cylinder

Type and physical dimensions
Material
Hot water capacity
Reheat period
Insulation
Anode

21.11 Electric Immersion Heater

Type and duty   kW
Control

21.12 Circulator

Make and type
Location

21.13 Feed & Expansion Cistern

Size
Location
Insulation

21.14 Sealed System Equipment

Expansion vessel size
Other equipment included
Working pressure
Safety valve discharge location

21.15 Programmers and Controls

Make, type and location
Programming facilities
Location of room and cylinder thermostat
Location of sensors

21.16 Electric Wiring

Specification of work included
Fused spur requirement and location
Size of fuse
Surface or concealed wiring

21.17 Pipework

Material
Type of fittings
Surface or concealed routing
Commissioning cleansing procedure and inhibitor chemicals to be used

21.18 Insulation

Material
Parts to be insulated
Thickness specification
Type of jointing

21.19 Corrosion Inhibitor

Type
Quantity

21.20 Building Work

Description of work included or excluded and required to be done by others

21.21 Waste and Scrap

Disposal of waste and scrap materials.

21.22 Variations to Contract

State how variations will be handled.

21.23 Commissioning and hand-Over procedure

State procedures and whether Benchmark scheme is operated.

21.24 Programme

Minimum time for installation to be carried out
Starting time, base on delivery of materials

21.25 Qualifications

Membership of professional bodies and trade associations:
APHC
CIBSE
HVCA
IDHE
IoP
SNIPEF

Always quote membership number

Registration with fuel bodies
CORGI (mandatory requirement for gas installations)
OFTEC (Competent Persons status for oil installations)

Always quote registration number.

21.26 Guarantees

Clearly state the guarantees
Enclose a copy of the terms of relevant guarantee schemes

21.27 Extended Warranty and Breakdown Insurance

State if operating the Benchmark scheme
Offer relevant Extended Warranty if applicable
Offer Service Contract if applicable
Offer relevant Breakdown Insurance if applicable

21.28 Health and Safety

Health and safety policy statement
COSHH details where applicable

21.29 Conditions of Contract

Terms for submission of invoices and payment

22.0 HAND OVER AND FUTURE SERVICE

22.1 System Operation Explained

The system should be fully operated and shown to work satisfactorily.

The winter and summer operation of the system and the controls should be clearly explained to the client with particular attention given to demonstrating the operation of the controls and how they are adjusted.

The client should also be instructed on how to light the boiler and shown the location of fuel shut-off valves and electrical fuses. Instructions should be given on the correct procedure for venting the system (with the pump off) and to re-balancing the circuits in the event of radiators having been removed for decoration etc.

22.2 Safety Instructions

It must be explained that air supply and fluing equipment must not be interfered with. Also that limit thermostats, bypass valves, safety valves and any other similar controls must not be tampered with.

22.3 Written Instructions

For all except the simplest control system, a written explanation of the operation should be given to the client. This may be best in the form of a diagrammatic layout similar to those in Section 18.

A full set of manufacturer's installation and operating instructions for all the equipment and a schedule of the equipment should be left on site for future reference.

22.4 Guarantees

Manufacturer's registration cards should be completed on behalf of the client and re-turned without delay.

Guarantees applying to the system and its component parts should be explained so that the customer is aware of the comprehensive guarantees which will be in force for the next twelve months covering workmanship, materials and performance, providing the conditions of the Guarantee are met

Any extended warranties to be offered should also be explained.

22.5 Benchmark

The 'Benchmark' scheme has been introduced to raise the standard of the installation, commissioning and servicing of central heating systems in the UK. Most new boilers should be supplied with a Benchmark logbook for the installer to complete and leave with the householder. The installer is required to sign the logbook to confirm that the boiler has been installed and commissioned following manufacturers instructions and also to complete a record of servicing. Householders should be encouraged to keep the logbook safely and to ensure that it is kept up to date when the boiler is serviced. The 'Benchmark' logbook should be passed on to the new owners if the property changes hands

22.6 Competent Persons Scheme

The Competent Persons scheme, which forms part of the Building Regulations in England and Wales, covers gas, oil and solid fuel appliance, heating system and fuel storage installation and commissioning work in new and existing houses. The scheme permits this work to be undertaken by persons classed as being competent, without the need to involve the Local Authority Building Control Department. The work must be covered by approved documentation. The documentation approved consists of the 'Benchmark' logbook, see above, and OFTEC forms CD/10 for oil firing installation work and CD/11 for oil firing commissioning work. This documentation should be kept by the householder to form a logbook record of work undertaken on the heating system which can be passed on to the new owners if the property changes hands.

22.7 Future Service

The client should be advised of the importance of entering into a regular service contract which will include visits by a competent service engineer, registered with CORGI or OFTEC as appropriate, to clean and maintain the boiler and check the operation of the controls.

Any heating appliance or heating system breakdown insurance which is available should then be explained.

The terms of the boiler manufacturer's warranty may require that system water checks are carried out.

22.8 Special Tools

At least two air vent keys, two fuses and any operating tools and spares that were supplied with the installed equipment should be handed to the client

23.0 SCHEDULE OF INSTALLED EQUIPMENT

23.1 Equipment Record

The Schedule of Installed Equipment should list all items of equipment, together with the operational settings of the controls.

Relevant information defining guarantee dates, extended insurance and service contracts, together with contact telephone numbers should also be given.

23.2 Record Drawings

If it has previously been agreed with the client, record drawings should be completed and accompany the schedule.

23.3 Emergency Contacts

Finally, the contact telephone number and the installer's name and address label should be fixed in a suitable position for easy reference, inside the boiler casing or at some other agreed location.

SCHEDULE OF INSTALLED EQUIPMENT

Client _____ Address _____ Job No. _____

ITEM	MANUFACTURER	TYPE or MODEL REF	SIZE	DUTY	WHERE FITTED	SETTING
Boiler		117f		11.7kW	Kitchen	Stat. 6
Pump		AZ/50			Airing cupboard	Speed 2
Programmer		CP850			Kitchen	As requested
3 way valve		mid position	22mm		Airing cupboard	-
Cylinder stat		32241/4			Cylinder	60 °C
Room stat		32261/1			Hall	18 °C
Cylinder		unvented	120ltr		Airing cupboard	-
Immersion heater		K3 with cut out	3kW		Cylinder	60 °C
Pressure vessel		3 ltr	3ltr		Kitchen	-
Safety valve		2A17	15mm	3 bar (fixed)	Kitchen	3 bar
Make-up bottle		3BB			Airing cupboard	FULL

see page 109 for reverse side

108

RADIATORS AND OTHER EMITTERS

ROOM	MAKE	SIZE	TRV
Lounge		S600 x 1500	Y
Kitchen/dining		D600 x 950	Y
Hall		D600 x 650	N
Bathroom		S600 x 650	Y
Bedroom 1		S500 x 1100	Y
Bedroom 2		S500 x 750	Y

Other instructions _____

The system has been left fully operational and working	YES	NO
The system has been drained down and we await your further instructions. The system fuse has been removed	YES	NO

A servicing contract for cleaning the boiler and maintaining the system HAS/HAS NOT been taken out as detailed below. Where a Service Contract has not been taken out an Application form is attached.

SERVICE CONTRACT

Annual Boiler Service	YES	NO
Annual full system check	YES	NO
OUR 12 MONTH GUARANTEE EXPIRES ON	21.11.01	
THE EXTENDED INSURANCE EXPIRES ON	21.11.05	
FIRST SERVICE IS DUE ON	21.11.01	

Insurance cover is conditional on the boiler and system being properly serviced in accordance with the manufacturer's instructions.

EMERGENCY TELEPHONE

OFFICE _____ MOBILE _____

NAME _____

COMPANY _____

ADDRESS _____

_____ Postcode _____

Reverse side of schedule

BUILDING REGULATIONS RELEVANT IN EACH COUNTRY

Subjects covered	England and Wales	Scotland	Northern Ireland	Republic of Ireland
Thermal insulation of building fabric, hot water storage and pipework, control of heating systems	Part L - The conservation of fuel and power	Part J - The conservation of fuel and power	Part F - The conservation of fuel and power	Part L - The conservation of fuel and energy
Provision of adequate ventilation for building occupants and control of condensation	Part F - Ventilation	Part K - Ventilation	Part K - Ventilation	Part F - Ventilation
Heat producing appliances; fuel storage	Part J - Heat producing appliances	Part F - Heat producing appliances and storage of liquid and gaseous fuels	Part L - Heat producing appliances and liquefied petroleum gas installations	Part J - Heat producing appliances
Unvented hot water storage	Part G - Hygiene	Part P - Miscellaneous hazards	Part P - Sanitary appliances and hot water storage systems	Part G - Hygiene (unvented HW storage effectively prohibited, as only the cold water supply to the kitchen sink may be connected directly to the mains water supply)

Building Legislation

In England and Wales, Building Regulations 2000 Part L1 (Conservation of fuel and power in dwellings), which came into effect in April 2002 and in Scotland, Building Standards (Scotland) Regulations Part J (Conservation of fuel and power) which came into effect in March 2002, place minimum standards of performance of energy efficiency on heating systems which designers must achieve. In England and Wales this now applies to replacement heating systems in existing housing as well as to new ones. Guidance on this is given in The Domestic Heating and Hot Water Guide to the Building Regulations 2001 – Part L1, published by the Energy Efficiency Partnership for Homes.

Gas Safety Legislation

All gas appliances and other gas fittings must be installed in accordance with the *Gas Safety (Installation and Use) Regulations*, which apply in England, Northern Ireland, Scotland and Wales. In particular it is required that all businesses, whether employers or self-employed persons, who undertake work on fittings supplied by Natural Gas be registered with a body approved by the Health and Safety Executive (HSE). The Council for registered Gas Installers (CORGI) was approved by the HSE for the purpose. In the Republic of Ireland, gas heating installations are covered by Irish Standard IS 813:1996 *Domestic gas installations*.

Water Legislation

Equipment connected directly to public water supplies in England and Wales must comply with the *Water Supply (Water Fittings) Regulations* (1999). Similar regulations apply in Northern Ireland, and in Scotland, through Water By-laws.

Boiler Efficiency Legislation

Boiler efficiency is controlled by *The Boiler (Efficiency) Regulations 1993* and *The Boiler (Efficiency) (Amendment) Regulations 1994*. The European Legislation is *Council Directive 92/42/EEC of 21 May 1992 on efficiency requirements for new hot-water boilers fired with liquid or gaseous fuels*.

Appendix B CONTROLS FOR DOMESTIC CENTRAL HEATING SYSTEMS - DEFINITIONS

B1 Time Switch

A switch operated by a clock to control either space heating or hot water, but not both. The user chooses one or more "on" periods, usually in a daily or weekly cycle.

B2 Programmer

Two switches operated by a clock to control both space heating and hot water. The user chooses one or more "on" periods, usually in a daily or weekly cycle. A **mini-programmer** allows space heating and hot water to be on together, or hot water alone. A **standard programmer** uses the same time settings for space heating and hot water. A **full programmer** allows the time settings for space heating and hot water to be fully independent.

B3 Room Thermostat

A sensing device to measure the air temperature within the building and switch on and off the space heating. A single target temperature may be set by the user.

B4 Night setback

A feature of a room thermostat that allows a lower temperature to be maintained outside the period during which the normal room temperature is required.

B5 Programmable Room Thermostat

A combined time switch and room thermostat which allows the user to set different periods with different target temperatures for space heating, usually in a daily or weekly cycle.

B6 Delayed Start

A device, or feature within a device, to delay the chosen starting time for space heating according to the temperature measured inside or outside the building.

B7   Optimum Start

A device, or feature within a device, to adjust the starting time for space heating according to the temperature measured inside or outside the building, aiming to heat the building to the required temperature by a chosen time.

B8   Optimum Stop

A device, or feature within a device, to adjust the stop time for space heating according to the temperature measured inside (and possibly outside) the building, aiming to prevent the required temperature of the building being maintained beyond a chosen time.

B9   Cylinder Thermostat

A sensing device to measure the temperature of the hot water cylinder and switch on and off the water heating. A single target temperature may be set by the user.

B10   Programmable Cylinder Thermostat

A combined time switch and cylinder thermostat which allows the user to set different periods with different target temperature for stored hot water, usually in a daily or weekly cycle.

B11   Weather Compensator

A device or feature within a device, which adjusts the temperature of water circulating through the heating system according to the temperature measured outside the building.

B12   Load Compensator

A device, or feature within a device, which adjusts the temperature of the water circulating through the heating system according to the temperature measured inside the building.

B13   Boiler Energy Manager

No agreed definition, but typically a device intended to improve boiler control using a selection of features such as weather compensation, load compensation, optimum start control, night setback, frost protection, anti-cycling control and hot water over-ride.

B14 Boiler anti-cycling Device

A device to introduce a time delay between boiler firing. Any energy saving is due to a reduction in performance of the heating system. The device does not provide boiler interlock.

B15 Boiler Thermostat

A thermostat within the boiler casing to limit the temperature of water passing through the boiler by switching off the boiler. The target temperature may either be fixed or set by the user.

B16 Boiler Auto Ignition

An electrically controlled device to ignite the boiler at the start of each firing, avoiding use of a permanent pilot flame.

B17 Boiler Modulator (water temperature)

A device, or feature within a device, to vary the fuel burning rate of a boiler according to measured water temperature. It is often fitted within the boiler casing. The boiler under control must have modulating capability.

B18 Boiler Modulator (air temperature)

A device, or feature within a device, to vary the fuel burning rate of a boiler according to measured room temperature. The boiler under control must have modulating capability and a suitable interface for connection.

B19 Pump Over-run

A timing device to run the heating system pump for a short period after the boiler stops firing to discharge very hot water from the boiler heat exchanger.

B20 Pump Modulator

A device to reduce pump power when not needed, determined by hydraulic or temperature conditions or firing status of the boiler.

B21 Motorised Valve

A valve to control water flow, operated electrically. A **2-port motorised valve** controls water flow to a single destination. A **3-port motorised valve** controls water flow to two destinations (usually for space heating and hot water), and may be either a **diverter valve** (only one outlet open at a time) or a **mid-position valve** (either one or both outlets open at a time). The valve movement may also open or close switches, which are used to control the boiler and pump.

B22 Automatic Bypass Valve

A valve to control water flow, operated by the water pressure across it. It is commonly used to maintain a minimum flow rate through a boiler and to limit circulation pressure when alternative water paths are closed (particularly in systems with thermostatic radiator valves).

B23 Thermostatic Radiator Valve

A radiator valve with an air temperature sensor, used to control the heat output from the radiator by adjusting water flow.

B24 Frost Thermostat

A device to detect low air temperature and switch on heating to avoid frost damage, arranged to over-ride other controls.

B25 Pipe Thermostat

A switch governed by a sensor measuring pipe temperature, normally used in conjunction with other controls such as a frost thermostat.

B26 Boiler Interlock

This is not a physical device but an arrangement of the system controls so as to ensure that the boiler does not fire when there is no demand for heat. In a system with a combi' boiler it can be achieved by fitting a room thermostat. In a system with a regular boiler it can be achieved by correct wiring interconnections between the room thermostat, cylinder thermostat and motorised valve(s). It may also be achieved by a suitable boiler energy manager.

B27 Zone Control

A control scheme in which it is possible to select different temperatures in two (or more) different zones.

B28 Temperature and Time Zone Control (or full zone control)

A control scheme in which it is possible to select different temperatures at different times in two (or more) different zones.

B29 Self-adaptive (or self-learning) control

A characteristic of a device (of various types) which learns from experience by monitoring, and modifies its subsequent behaviour accordingly.

Appendix C STANDARDS AND GUIDANCE DOCUMENTS RELATING TO DOMESTIC HEATING INSTALLATIONS

C1 British Standards

BS 799:1987	Oil burning equipment
	Part 5 Specification for oil storage tanks
BS 1566:2002	Copper indirect cylinders for domestic premises
BS 2869:1998	Specification for fuel oil for agricultural, domestic and industrial engines and boilers
BS 3198:1981	Specification for copper hot water storage combination units for domestic premises
BS 4814:1990	Specification for expansion vessels using an internal diaphragm, for sealed hot water heating systems
BS 5250:1989	Code of practice: control of condensation in buildings
BS 5410	Code of practice for oil firing
	Part 1:1997 Installations up to 45kW output capacity for space heating and hot water supply purposes
BS 5422:1990	Methods for specifying thermal insulation materials on pipes, ductwork and equipment in the temperature range of -40°C to +700°C
BS 5440	Installation and maintenance of flues and ventilation for gas appliances of rated input not exceeding 70kW nett (1st and 2nd family gases)
	Part 1:1990 Specification for installation of flues
	Part 2:2000 Specification for installation and maintenance of ventilation
BS 5970:1992	Code of practice for thermal insulation of pipework and equipment
BS 6351:1983	Electric surface heating. Specification for electric surface heating devices
BS 6700:1997	Specification for design, installation, testing and maintenance of services supplying water for domestic use within buildings and their curtilages
BS 6798:2000	Specification for installation of gas-fired boilers of rated output not exceeding 70kW nett
BS 7074	Application, selection and installation of expansion vessels and ancillary equipment for sealed water systems
	Part 1:1989 Code of practice for domestic heating and hot water supply
BSEN1264:1998	Floor Heating Systems and Components
BS ISO EN 13370	Thermal performance of buildings. Heat transfer via the ground. Calculation methods
BS7593:1992	The Code of Practice for: Treatment of water in domestic hot water central heating systems
BSEN12828:2003	Heating systems in buildings – Design for water based heating systems

C2 CIBSE Publications

Guide A – Environmental Design

C3 CORGI Publications

Essential Gas Safety

C4 Energy Efficiency Best Practice Programme Publications

Good Practice Guide 143:	Upgrading controls in domestic wet central heating systems - a guide for installers
Good Practice Guide 284:	Domestic central heating and hot water: systems with gas and oil fired boilers - guidance for installers and specifier
Good Practice Guide 302:	Controls for domestic heating and hot water systems
General Information Leaflet 83:	Domestic boiler anti-cycling controls
Other publications:	Whole house boiler sizing method
	How to choose an efficient boiler - CHESS

C5 HVCA Publications

TR5	Welding of Carbon Steel Pipework
TR6	Guide to Good Practice – Site Pressure Testing of Pipework
TR11	Guide to the use of plastic pipework
TR20	Installation and Testing of Pipework Systems

C6 IoP Publications

Plumbing Engineering Services Guide

C7 OFTEC Publications

OFS T100 Oil Fired Equipment Standard -	Polyethylene oil storage tanks for distillate fuels (Edition 2 2002)
OFS T200 Oil Fired Equipment Standard -	Steel oil storage tanks and tank bunds for use with distillate fuels, lubrication oils and waste oils (Edition 3 2002)
OFS E101 Oil Fired Equipment Standard -	Remote acting fire safety valves for use with oil supply systems (1998)
OFS E103 Oil Fired Equipment Standard -	Gauges for use with oil supply tanks (2000)
OFS E104 Oil Fired Equipment Standard -	Filters and water separators for use with oil supply systems (2001)
OFS E105 Oil Fired Equipment Standard -	Overfill alarms and overfill prevention devices for use with oil supply tanks (2001)
OFS E106 Oil Fired Equipment Standard -	Flues for use with oil fired boilers with outputs not above 50kW (2001)
Technical Information Book Three:	Installation requirements for oil fired equipment (Edition 9 April 2002)
Technical Information Book Four:	System design and operating principles (Edition 4 2002)
Technical Information Note TI/112:	Oil fired appliances and extract fans (Issue 0.4 April,2002)
Technical Information Note TI/120:	Oil storage inspection and maintenance (Issue 2 2002)
Technical Information Note TI/129:	Advice on flues for modern open flued oil fired boilers (Issue 0.2 2001)
Technical Information Note TI/131:	Siting of Class 1 type oil tanks for single family dwellings (Issue 4 Jun. 2001)
Technical Information Note TI/132:	Air supply requirements (Issue 0.3 August 2001)
Technical Information Note TI/133:	Assessment of the risk of environmental damage being caused by spillage from domestic oil storage tanks (Issue 0.9 2002)
Technical Information Note TI/134:	Installing oil supply pipes underground (Issue 0.2 July 2001)
Technical Information Note TI/135:	Positioning of flue terminations (Issue 0.2 Oct. 2001)
Technical Information Note TI/136:	Fire protection of oil storage tanks (Issue 0.3 Mar.2002)
Technical Information Note TI/138:	Positioning of fire valves (2001)
Technical Information Note TI/139:	Installation of top outlet fuel oil storage tanks and suction oil supply pipe sizing (May 2002)

Appendix D. CONVERSION FACTORS

D1   Conversion Squares

Conversion squares enable you to convert in either direction between Imperial and S.I. units and to other units within the same system. Select initial unit and then move round the square, multiplying by the factor if the arrow points in your direction of travel, or by dividing if it points towards you.

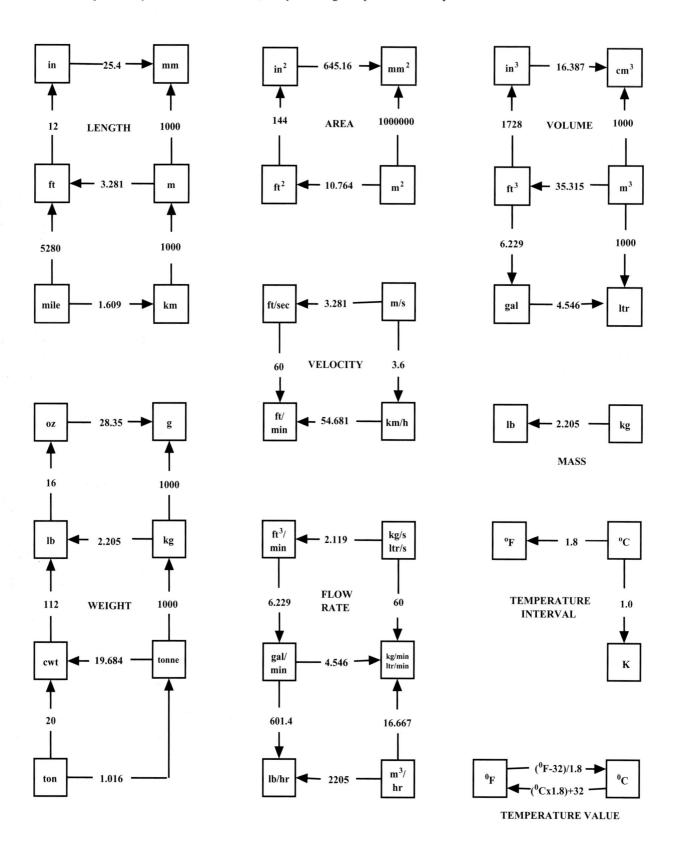

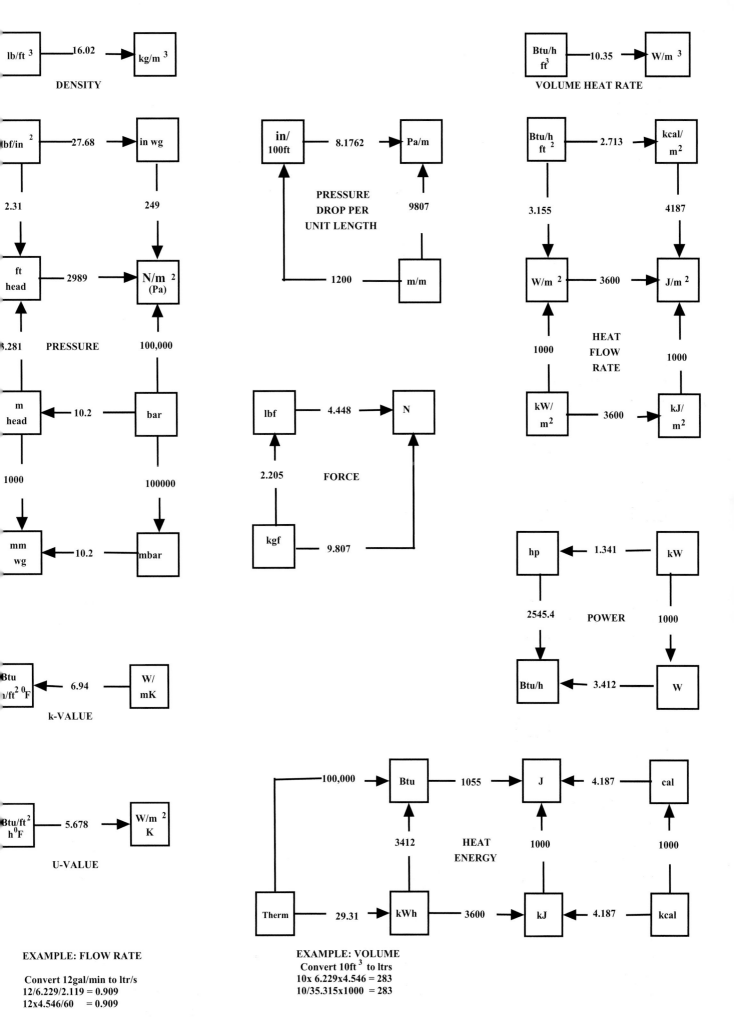

DENSITY

VOLUME HEAT RATE

PRESSURE DROP PER UNIT LENGTH

PRESSURE

FORCE

HEAT FLOW RATE

POWER

k-VALUE

U-VALUE

HEAT ENERGY

EXAMPLE: FLOW RATE

Convert 12gal/min to ltr/s
12/6.229/2.119 = 0.909
12x4.546/60   = 0.909

EXAMPLE: VOLUME
Convert 10ft^3 to ltrs
10x 6.229x4.546 = 283
10/35.315x1000 = 283

119

Appendix E DETAILS OF ORGANISATIONS FROM WHOM THIS GUIDE IS AVAILABLE

E1 Heating and Ventilating Contractors' Association

Esca House
34 Palace Court
Bayswater
London
W2 4JG

☎ 020 7313 4900
Fax: 020 7727 9268
Website: www.hvca.org.uk

Publications Department
Old Mansion House
Eamont Bridge
Penrith
Cumbria CA10 2BX

☎ 01768 860400
Fax: 01768 860401

E2 Chartered Institution of Building Services Engineers

222 Balham High Road
Balham
London
SW12 9BS

☎ 020 8675 5211
Fax: 020 8675 5449
Website: www.cibse.org

E3 Association of Plumbing and Heating Contractors

Unit 14, Ensign House
Ensign Business Centre
Westwood Way
Coventry
West Midlands CV4 8JA

☎ 024 7647 0626
Fax: 024 7647 0942
Website: www.aphc.co.uk

E4 Heating and Hotwater Information Council

36 Holly Walk
Leamington Spa
Warwickshire CV32 4LY

☎ 0845 600 2200
Fax: 01926 423 284
Website: www.centralheating.co.uk

E5 CORGI Services

1 Elmwood
Chineham Business Park
Crockford Lane
Basingstoke
Hants
RG24 8WG

☎ 01256 372200
Fax: 01256 708144
Website: www.mainserve.demon.co.uk/page3.htm

E6 Institute of Domestic Heating & Environmental Engineers

Dorchester House
Wimblestraw Road
Berinsfield
Wallingford
OX10 7LZ

☎ 01865 343096
Fax: 01865 340181
Website: www.idhe.org.uk

E7 Institute of Plumbing

64 Station Lane
Hornchurch
Essex
RM12 6NB

☎ 01708 472791
Fax: 01708 448987
Website: www.plumbers.org.uk

E8 Oil Firing Technical Association (OFTEC)

Foxwood House
Dobbs Lane
Kesgrave
Ipswich
IP5 2QQ

☎ 0845 6585080
Fax: 0845 6585181
Website: www.oftec.org

E9 Scottish and Northern Ireland Plumbing Employers Federation

2 Walker Street
Edinburgh
EH3 7LB

☎   0131 225 2255
Fax: 0131 226 7638
Website: www.snipef.org

Appendix F   BLANK COPIES OF THE WORKSHEETS USED IN THIS BOOK

The following pages contain blank versions of the worksheets used in this book.

DOMESTIC HEATING DESIGN GUIDE

WORKSHEET ONE – HEAT LOSSES

ROOM						Page	
	No. of air changes per hour ach	Room volume *Enter measurements*			Amount of air to be heated per hour *Calculate* m³/hour	*Enter factor*	Heat loss/°C *Calculate* W/K
		Length m	Width m	Height m			
VENTILATION HEAT LOSS						x 0.33 =	
FABRIC HEAT LOSS					Area m²	U-value W/m²K	
FLOOR							
WALL							
GLAZING (U = Glazing U - Wall U)							
DOOR (U = Door U - Wall U)							
ROOF							
ROOF GLAZING (U = Glazing U - Wall U)							
OTHER 1							
PARTY WALL (U = ½ of tabulated value)							

DESIGN ROOM TEMPERATURE			TOTAL HEAT LOSS/°C (W/K) *(sum of above)*	
– OUTSIDE TEMPERATURE				
= TEMPERATURE DIFFERENCE		→	x TEMPERATURE DIFFERENCE °C	
			= DESIGN HEAT LOSS (W)	
EXPOSED LOCATION?		If yes, add	% to design heat loss (see 8.5)	
HIGH CEILING?		If yes, add	% to design heat loss (see 8.6)	
INTERMITTENT HEATING Add			% to design heat loss (see 8.8)	
			Total room heat loss W *(enter on Worksheet 3)*	

DOMESTIC HEATING DESIGN GUIDE WORKSHEET TWO – EMISSION FACTORS	
Boiler flow temperature (T_F)	
System temperature drop (ΔT)	
Mean water temperature (MWT = $T_F - (\Delta T/2)$)	
Design room temperature (T_R)	
Temperature difference (T_D = MWT $- T_R$)	
f1 *(from table 10.1)*	
f2 *(from table 10.2)*	
f3 *(from table 10.3)*	
f4 *(from table 10.4)*	
f = f1 x **f2** x **f3** x **f4** *(Enter on Worksheet Three)*	

DOMESTIC HEATING DESIGN GUIDE
WORKSHEET THREE – RADIATOR SELECTION

Room	Design temp °C	Heat losses (from Work-sheet One) W	Pipework emissions (from Work-sheet Four) W	Nett heat output required from radiator (heat losses minus pipework emissions) W	Emission factor f (from Worksheet Two) W	Radiator listed output required (nett heat output divided by emission factor) W	Radiator selection (from catalogue)	Catalogue listed output W	Actual calculated output (catalogue output multiplied by emission factor) W
Totals W									

DOMESTIC HEATING DESIGN GUIDE
WORKSHEET FOUR – EXPOSED PIPEWORK EMISSIONS

| Room | Temp. diff. (water to air) °C | Pipe Emission | | | | Total pipe emission (PE) W |
		Size mm	Length (L) m	Output (from Table 10.5) W/m	Location factor f_5 (from Table 10.6)	

DOMESTIC HEATING DESIGN GUIDE
WORKSHEET FIVE – BOILER SIZING

Boiler size calculation	Watts
Total heat loss from rooms	
Distribution losses (add 10% if required)	
Hot water allowance (from Table 12.1)	
Total heat load to be met by boiler	

DOMESTIC HEATING DESIGN GUIDE

WORKSHEET SIX – FLOW RATE AND PIPE SIZE

Room	Radiator output required *(from work- sheet three)* W	Emiss- ions from exposed pipe W	Combined output from radiators and exposed pipe W	10% heat loss from mains W	Total heat loss W	Flow rate kg/s	Initially selected pipe diameter mm

Revisions

DOMESTIC HEATING DESIGN GUIDE
WORKSHEET SEVEN – PRESSURE LOSS

Pipe section	Flow rate kg/s	Selected pipe diameter mm	Length of flow and return pipes in metres m	Pressure loss in metres per metre run m/m	Total pressure loss metres head m	Comments
			Index circuit Sub. total			
Flow rate sub. total			Allowance for fittings 50% of sub. total			
Add bypass (if fitted)			Other allowances			
Total flow rate		kg/s	**Total pressure loss**		**Metres head**	

DOMESTIC HEATING DESIGN GUIDE
WORKSHEET EIGHT – WATER CONTENT OF SYSTEM

Component					Water content litres
Boiler	Manufacturer and type	Output kW	Water content *(from manufacturer's literature)* *Enter in end column*		
Cylinder	Manufacturer and type	Size litres	Water content of coil *(from manufacturer's literature)* *Enter in end column*		

Pipework	Diameter mm	Length m	Water content per metre litres		
	8		0.036		
	10		0.055		
	15		0.145		
	22		0.320		
	28		0.539		
	35		0.835		
	42		1.232		

Heat emitters	Location	Type *(SP,DP DPC, etc.)*	Height mm	No. of sections or length	Water content per section or length *(from manufacturer's literature)* litres	
					Total system water content	

EXPANSION VESSEL SELECTION

Static pressure of water above expansion vessel (cold) bar	Total system water content litres	Safety valve setting bar	**Vessel selected** *(from manufacturer's catalogue)*	
			Vessel charge and initial system fill pressure bar	Vessel volume litres

SCHEDULE OF INSTALLED EQUIPMENT

Client _____ Address _____ Job No. _____ Page 1 of 2

ITEM	MANUFACTURER	TYPE or MODEL REF	SIZE	DUTY	WHERE FITTED	SETTING

RADIATORS AND OTHER EMITTERS

ROOM	MAKE	SIZE	TRV

ROOM	MAKE	SIZE	TRV

	YES	NO
The system has been left fully operational and working		
The system has been drained down and we await your further instructions. The system fuse has been removed		

Other instructions _____

A servicing contract for cleaning the boiler and maintaining the system HAS/HAS NOT been taken out as detailed below. Where a Service Contract has not been taken out an Application form is attached.

SERVICE CONTRACT

	YES	NO
Annual Boiler Service		
Annual full system check		

OUR 12 MONTH GUARANTEE EXPIRES ON

THE EXTENDED INSURANCE EXPIRES ON

FIRST SERVICE IS DUE ON

Insurance cover is conditional on the boiler and system being properly serviced in accordance with the manufacturer's instructions.

EMERGENCY TELEPHONE

OFFICE _____ MOBILE _____

NAME _____

COMPANY _____

ADDRESS _____

Postcode _____

Reverse side of schedule